Change Your Circle, Change Your Life

By Jamar Jones

TABLE OF CONTENTS

DEDICATED TO:

my Mom, Allison Jones and my Dad, Mayo Jones

my beautiful better half, Cristina Ferreira

my loving Grandpa may he now rest in peace - Linwood Jones Jr.

my amazing Grandma Emma, rest in peace - Emma Jones

my wise Granddaddy, rest his soul - Otha Jones

ACKNOWLEDGMENTS

Randy Wilinski and Marissa Ray for helping
me pull this book off!

Cory Kroll • Stephen Crofford aka Plex

Book Coach - Cathy Fyock • Amy C Waginger

Rick Hartline • Marcus Lemonis aka The Profit

Colleen Sullivan • Rashod Jones

James Bowens • Sarah Jones

Jeff Kortes • Casey Kroll

All the amazing Design work for the book: Ali Andruss

Brett McManus • Carlos Caraballo

My Haters :)

Uncle Lamont • Grandma Effie

Viviana Ferreira • Sky McCloud

Promise (P-Rock) Bruce • Jasmine Jones

Aunt JoJo • Uncle Lewis

Nieces and Nephews • Foureva Media Team

CONTENTS AND INTERACTION

MESSAGE FROM JAMAR JONES

This book has many elements to it that I really want you to immerse yourself with and create action.

I wanted this to be unique experience and learn from different methods. There is music that goes along with each chapter in the book. They are all original songs that created!

To get access to the music and song list please visit www.iamjamarjones.com

Join our growing Facebook Group Community at https://www.facebook.com/groups/788004555239801/

Check for new updates on www.iamjamarjones.com for workbooks, workshops, assessments and tools to help you Change your Circle.

Audio book version will be available as well on www.iamjamarjones.com

Use the tools to help with your situation to reach success.

Change your Circle, Change your Life
The How to Guide to Change Anyone's Life

Copyright © 2021 by Jamar Jones

Jamar Jones
www.iamjamarjones.com

Library of Congress Cataloging-in-Publication Data
ISBN 978-1-7371919-0-2 (Paperback)
ISBN 978-1-7371919-1-9 (E-book)

Cover by Ali Andruss
Typesetting by Cal Sharp at www.caligraphics.net

☼ OPENING ☼

Change Your Circle, Change Your Life is a direct lifestyle that needs to be applied continuously for any human being to be successful. Through these chapters, you will go through so many mental and physical shifts that will challenge you as a human being. The purpose of this philosophy is to enhance your lifestyle and promote your growth. The more circles you touch, the more lives you can change. Following the methods in the book will transform your excuses into results. I would not be where I am today if it wasn't for this mindset and the actions, I took to constantly change my circles and meet new people. It actually manipulated my framework of thought, direction, purpose, connection. and faith.

A circle can be your personal circle like your friends, family, and acquaintances. Or your business circle like your coworkers, close business relationships, and mentors. Your circle affects more decisions than you know. This book is a guide to help you navigate through life. Once you take these principles and make them real in your life, you will then be able to make it real in the lives of others. That means you're going to give someone else a fighting chance. This book is important because it contains raw and realistic action items, activities and suggestions that anyone can do. This book comes from a place of 50% mindset and 50% action from someone who is just like you. A lot of other books don't dive into an actionable, step-by-step, realistic program that you can actually start today with results that are big enough to impact your current situation at the highest level.

This program will change your life because it changed mine. I had no special skills, no handouts, no sail with wind to carry me to where I had to go. Participating in various circles was the key to unlocking my mindset and then opportunities. If you follow the ideas in this book, you will increase the opportunities to change your life.

Are you ready?

☼ How I See It ☼

It's all how you see it, then you can create it.

Perspective is a mindset about how you handle and attack situations. Perspective is a lens that you need to put on. A lot of people don't look at different perspectives. Perspective can set you up for everything. The less perspective you have (a narrow view, one-sided view) the more likely you are to lose. You're not going to get where you're trying to go anytime soon. Perspective defines your outlook on every situation. The wider perspective you have and the more open you are to new ideas and experiences, the more you can take in.

People will always ask, "Why do you care what they think?"

Seek to understand, not to be understood.

Try to understand where they're coming from. Even the haters. You have to take that perspective and react accordingly. Most people are narrowminded and not open.

I grew up in a diverse community and gained a perspective from many different world views and ideas. These varying mindsets gave me a different perspective. And perspective can drive you to results.

I look at issues that affect me and events that happen around me and my perspective is so wide I don't just look at my own opinion. This openness outrages people and I really wonder why. People are looking at their life and the world from a very narrow lens. You gain perspective when you place yourself in a situation and you make it about "we, we, we, we" instead of "me, me, me, me," You need to have self-awareness. You don't gain perspective from assumptions or what a few people have taught you. You need to build a wider perspective.

For instance, somebody's perspective on something might be, "I don't want to go talk to those rich folks. I don't like those rich jerks over there because they're pompous and full of themselves." Another example is when former gang members visit schools and speak to students. Some people might say, "Oh, I don't want to associate with that or those people. I've seen that type in movies that they're horrible people."

You're speaking from a limited perspective. It could be a time to understand and not necessarily to be understood. You need to ask questions instead of making assumptions to form beliefs.

A closed perspective limits your ability to change your circle.

My environment changed my perspective forever from just one job...

Now that I'm a business owner, my perspective is much, much wider than it was prior to opening my company. Prior to that and before I started at PLS, a financial service retailer company, my It was a job I had in IT doing software support and management. Before I knew about corporate America and the politics that go on once you start to climb up the ladder, my perspective was honestly very shallow. I never questioned where my paychecks came from or how they got to me. I never considered the action going on behind the scenes. All I knew was, I got my check mailed to me and I cashed that bad boy.

Even at PLS in the beginning, I didn't second guess my paychecks. What if it doesn't show up? How did it get here? Can I get more? Eventually years passed and I started seeing how leadership works in different departments. What is the real money driver in the company? Who is making the power plays? There were all of these corporate politics going on.

Looking back, I understand why our Brookfield location was laid off. Roughly 45 people just boom! lost their jobs because our new fancy VP of IT sold a dream to the executives that he could save the

3

company more money. Our Brookfield office was always kind of the scapegoat because we weren't down in Chicago where the main headquarters was located. So, there was always this fear of what if they don't want this office in Brookfield anymore? What if they want to consolidate the offices and have a more central location?

I started to see that our support department was really needed while we were expendable. We were one of the first departments in line to get cut. When I got laid off at PLS, I thought, "They can't just do me like that?" My perspective was so locked into and focused on one area, I couldn't see the bigger picture. My perspective on how strings are pulled was so narrow compared to my understanding now. I look at things differently.

To change your circle, you need to change your perspective. A stubborn, closed mindset will not help you change your circle. On the flip side, your perspective is going to constantly change. It doesn't matter--good or bad--your perspective will change.

Learning a different perspective shows you which circles to be in. If you're a tier 1 sales rep, a janitor, or what is often considered a "lower-end" position in your company, you're at a higher risk for something to happen to your position if layoffs occur. You have to evaluate the perspective. For example, at PLS when the whole office got laid off, if I had aligned myself differently the outcome could have been different.

For example, I eventually aligned myself with Cory Kroll, a development manager at PLS who is now a good friend of mine. He added so much value to the executives that after the layoffs were done, they brought him back to do consulting work. Make sure you make yourself a person, not a number. By time you finish this book you will achieve this flawlessly.

You need to place yourself into the circle of the decision makers. I only knew a few people at PLS who could've gotten me into those circles.

There are many layers to perspective, mindset, expectations, and accountability. When you open your perspective, you can evaluate where you're at and what you can expect. **Gaining perspective is a cycle that includes these steps.**

1. Gaining perspective. Looking out for different viewpoints and listening to why. It's important to put your beliefs to the side here and focus on the understanding.

2. What's the value? Why is that new perspective you just learned, valued? Once again, put your beliefs to the side and ask questions in a curious way.

3. Having personal accountability. Ask yourself how can I take personal responsibility for this and change/affect my current situation.

4. Evaluate the current situation. This is when you will now evaluate the new perspective to your own beliefs. Learn here and grow from the new found knowledge.

5. Analyze and explore opportunity. Look at this as an opportunity of change and how can I learn to grow or better my own situation.

6. Realize the expectations. Important to see your beliefs before and after to understand the expectations of YOU moving forward.

Then start again with gaining perspective.

Perspective is an actionable task that requires an adjustment to your personal beliefs and your mindset. Act on it.

Travel can be one of the fastest ways to unlock your perspective...

I grew up in America and had living there all of my life. I had traveled to different states and seen different things but had never been outside of the country

Change Your Circle, Change Your Life

My stomach was in knots traveling to a new country. When I got there and that plane landed, I was seeing things I'd never seen before. The building structures were different from America as they looked more dated, houses very close together, and dated. Also, there were multiple languages being spoken right on the same street. From Spanish, to African, to Italian and Portuguese. So amazing to see this unfold right in front of me. At Heathrow Airport, the bathrooms were called toilets. Everything was different. Now I was the one who was different. From there on, I started to learn. I'm the foreigner now. I'm not used to any of this, where I'm at, or where I need to go. Just seeing the city, how people interact, etc. In London I didn't get "the look" I get here in America as a Black man. In this new place, I didn't get any of those prejudged stares and attention.

My first few days there, my mind was just blown. I felt both high and drunk at the same time (I wasn't either). The city looked completely different than what I was used to. People took the bus commonly. There were so many different cultures. I remember seeing a woman walking the city in a full hijab and shopping in a store. No one batted an eye at her differences.

By the second day, as I was looking out the window from my hotel room, I realized that my whole perspective had changed. My mind had opened to new possibilities. That was the first time I had truly seen a melting pot. It was incredible to see that diversity.

I had no idea what I was doing, how to take the bus, how to pay for things, or even cross the street. Also, I got to experience the locals' views on my homeland of America. No one knew where Milwaukee was, so I just referenced Chicago. I didn't cut them off or try to correct them mid-sentence. I was taking that opportunity to learn and listen. It was fascinating. The takeaways were priceless. One of the biggest takeaways that my world isn't as big as I thought it was. All I knew was the USA. It forced me to think global and what that meant for me.

After one week, I returned to Chicago. As soon as I got back. I got those stares again. If you are a minority in the US, you will know exactly what I'm talking about. If not, it is a stare at someone like "why are you here?" "Or are you lost?" Could even be a troubled stare as if there was something to worry about. I was just shaking my head like, "I guess I'm back home!" Unbelievable.

I have noticed that people are so freaked out about the littlest things. The world is so much larger and more gigantic than the little world view that they are used to in their own personal islands. You need to see different cultures, understand where others are coming from.

Never Worry Until you need to Worry….

Change Your Circle, Change Your Life

Cristina is my partner in crime. She is my right-hand woman that I love and cherish. She is our creative genius at Foureva Media but also my loving supportive partner.

There was one time, Cristina Ferreira and I were walking through IKEA in Minnesota and I lost my keys. When we got to the car, I couldn't unlock it. I was like, "Oh shoot, I lost the keys. Let's go retrace our steps. Let's leave the stuff under the car and behind the wheels."

She asked, "Why aren't you freaking out about this?" I said, "What is there to worry about?" We don't need to worry until we really need to worry."

We were still looking for the keys at this point. The store wasn't closed so I knew it would be better to keep a clear mind than to panic. After rummaging through the store for about 30 minutes we finally found the keys next to a light fixture display. No one had stolen them. We picked them up and went on with our day.

Ever since that moment, Cristina has not panicked right away when things like this happen. The panic doesn't start until she really needs to worry about it. She knows that in the grand scheme of things, she's going to get through this. The only way to change your perspective is to open your mind to new experiences.

With perspective you gain gratitude and appreciation for what you have and the opportunities that are in front of you. With greater gratitude comes greater opportunities.

You don't have to go to London to change your perspective. Find a new favorite store in the inner city. Try a new cuisine or restaurant. Visit a few new places downtown. If you live in the inner, metropolitan part of the city, it's only about twenty minutes away from a suburb usually. Travel there and check it out.

Go to a mall in a new town, join a Facebook group, go to an event somewhere you've never been. Challenge your perspective because the wider your lens, the more you can see, and the more opportunities you'll have to grow. If you're only looking through the tiny straw hole, you will get comfortable and stop learning.

You need to be consistently learning and pushing yourself until your last breath. Otherwise, you're pushing yourself to a disadvantage.

Change Your Circle, Change Your Life

Lessons and Takeaway

Perspective is a lens you have to put on. A lot of people don't exercise looking at others' perspectives. If you only see your own perspective, you're not going to get anywhere you're trying to go anytime soon. Perspective determines your outlook in every situation. The more you experience, the more you can take in.

Seek to understand, not to be understood, even from someone you might deem as a hater. Most people are narrowminded and not too open.

- Practice self-awareness.
- Build a wider perspective.
- Take time to understand and not be necessarily understood.
- Ask questions instead of forming assumptions.

Action Items

Step 1 - Understand your own perspective. Widen your view. You will limit your circle if you keep only one lens and only understand people in your circle. You may hear things that you may not know about or that make you uncomfortable but set aside your biases, preset assumptions, and misunderstanding of different cultures. Make sure you're willing to learn. You limit your options if you don't step out of your own shoes. Look from the top down and see the big picture. Don't only zoom in on things that you believe and understand. You will grow more, learn, and flourish if you keep your mindset open.

Step 2 - Get out of your comfort zone. A lot of people who never leave their neighborhood assume that everywhere else in the world is similar. Leave your city, leave your country, leave your comfort zone. If you don't have the vacation and gas to physically leave your town or city, don't make money an excuse or a crutch. You can use YouTube, Facebook, do volunteer work at a shelter. Visit museums or exhibits that are free. Help build a home with Habitat for Humanity. Get a someone you can trust's opinion on your options and then form a decision from that.

Step 3 - Spend five minutes jotting down everything you'd like to better understand. "I wonder how that works. I wonder how that is." Sports, cultures, people, it could be anything. Write down what may interest you.

Step 4 - Spend another five minutes writing down things you do *not* want to take the time to understand. This is where your strong beliefs are. Find the individuals who are in those spaces. Don't look at it as changing your perspective. Widen your perspective. Be prepared for your thoughts to change. You're more educated now and are more easily able to change your circles.

Step 5 - Spend another five minutes identifying beliefs that are different than yours and write them down. Research each belief online or directly ask someone you know you can talk to. Now when you go into those conversations make sure you have this quote in mind: "Speak to understand, not to be understood." Become a sponge. Say nothing; do nothing. Leave your biases at the door. Don't join a group that you want to learn more about to be a jerk. Soak it in. Observe. You're a visitor. Go directly to the source. Spend fifteen minutes on each.

Step 6 - Pick one destination that is in a completely different environment than what you're used to. Go to it and spend half a day there. It could be a different city, or it could be a different country (you would spend more than a half a day here). Go somewhere out of your comfort zone. If you're from the countryside, spend half a day in the city. If there is a barrier of travel, be creative. Figure out a way to get there. Become immersed in that community during that half day. Try their food, check out their communities, sightsee. Become a local. Just like you'd travel on a vacation, do it in your hometown as well. If you live in inner-city Milwaukee, for instance, travel to a new city. You can go alone, but having a "tour guide" that is already familiar with the place is helpful.

Reflection: Keep a journal of things that you've learned.

☼ LIFE'S NOT FAIR; YOU ☼ HAVE TO EVEN OUT THE ODDS

What if you could even out the chances to success?

I always thought life's not fair; you have to even out the odds. To have expectations of life or that you should be doing this, or this is how it should happen, I don't think that way. I always disagree with the statement, "It's a human right to get this or that." Everything is debatable; and I am always open for a debate. Just think about this for a moment. When you think about life, that's your life. All you can control is your life. Life's not fair or for anyone else. Even people who seem to have everything get screwed in a different capacity at some point. It's crazy to ever think something should be handed to them. It all evens out.

The real question you should ask yourself is, how do you not leave it up to chance? How do I take life, which I'm expecting to not b e a perfect fairy tale, and even out the odds so that I have a fighting chance?

To do that you must first have the mindset: Nothing is owed to you. You have to work for everything. Yes, everything.

Even when approached by Police, your response is everything...

It was one evening when I was 21, when my mind switched to "Okay, I need to play the safe route. I need to adjust the way I'm living to even out the odds." That was the evening when I got arrested for supposedly stealing gas; that was life just screwing me over. I was not actually stealing gas. It was late (midnight-ish) and I was just pumping gas like everyone else. My friend was visiting from out of town; he got out from the passenger side to talk to me at the pump. Then we got back in the car and drove off. Normal, right?!

Change Your Circle, Change Your Life

It should be but I got chased by the gas station owner who was behind me and almost chased me off the road. I didn't know it was him at the time. I thought it was some crazy driver who had had too much to drink. Who knows what would happen if I pulled over and gave him a piece of my mind? I didn't know he was even from the gas station and I was trying to lose him. I almost did, when suddenly I see lights flashing and I get pulled over by the police. For the first time in my life, I was happy to see the police! I told him I was so happy to see him.

He asked me what was going on. I told him I was just trying to go home, and a crazy dude was trying to run me off the road. He goes over to the other car to talk to the guy who was following me. He came back to me and was like, "Sir, do you know why I pulled you over?" Then he answered his own question: "The car behind you is actually the owner of the gas station you just left and he said you stole gas from there." I felt shocked and slighted in that moment. **The crazy thing is I actually paid the gas that night. You'll see what happened later.**

First, I was making plenty enough money to pay for the $20 or however much it was. The cop told me I stole gas. I was presented with an issue.

Stop right here in the story. This moment is critical. Life's not fair and you have a decision to make. You can act like you're owed, and life is supposed to be fair. Throw a tantrum and complain till your face falls off. Or you can ask, how can I even this out? I can't help my skin color. I have no proof of purchase and the whole situation was not fair. I had a decision to make. I could've yelled at the police or taken another negative approach.

Back to the Story. I said "Alright." I stated my case twice in a calm manner. I tried to handle any encounter with the police cordially and set it up for my success. Even my friend was like. "What are you talking about?" to the police. I told him that I can go pay for this right now. I just filled up my tank. And so he goes back to the car and says that the guy wants to press charges. "Get out of the vehicle." The whole situation was not fair. I had a decision and made the decision to say it'll all work out. I wanted to flatten it out. I'm a Black male, at night in the middle of the night, with another Black friend and someone said I stole gas, which is a federal offense.

So I got out of the car, they cuffed me, they put me in the back seat, and I'm on my way to the station. I got questioned and the guy checking me in told me I should be fine. Luckily enough a few months later the case was dropped. The craziest thing was that the gas pump had malfunctioned multiple times with other people!

The judge said "They need to fix the pump; it's happened before." Don't expect life to give you these expectations that you feel you're owed. You have to even it out. There will be times when you will have to decide. And that decision is everything.

The world can paint any picture it wants. It's up to you how you see and interact with that picture.

Everyone has things about themselves that they cannot control or change. It is out of their reach. We are going to dive into a couple of ways that you can think about and react to those situations.

To my brothers and my sisters. This is for everyone. Can we talk about it? Can we talk about it? We are all human beings and there is only one race and that's the human race.

With that being said, I understand the landscape that we are in and I'm going to be talking from the experiences of a Black man in America. If you are from a different walk of life, then this is a time to take notes, listen, and understand. A lot of the things that I will be talking about you can apply to your life as well. Everyone has things stacked against them. Could be a financial situation, born into poverty, parents that are not supportive, systematic issues in society, there are so many examples I could give. How do you maneuver around those challenges? How much do you need to act on them?

Imagine this: Everyone thought that life is unfair and there is nothing they can do. They accept the fact that there's nothing they can do. With this attitude, we would've never made the advances that we've made so far from the great people paving the way. People who have helped the next generation get just a little bit further ahead. My Dad, my Uncle Lamont, and my Aunt Linda were the first in our immediate family to attend and graduate college. Through all of the adversities, roadblocks, and challenges, they were the first to pave the way and show it was possible. This is just an example of the leaps we can take by not surrendering to the challenges. It's about rising up over the occasion and becoming more.

Back to my brothers and my sisters of color in America... We all know that, a lot of the time, we use the color of our skin as a reason or excuse for why we are not able to achieve something. The truth is, there are things stacked up against people who are not the majority. Oftentimes, I see that even within our own communities and circles we use our skin color as a scapegoat as to why we are not able to achieve certain things. As if there are evil people and evil things that are preventing us from achieving certain heights. One of the truths is, it's hard to see what is possible when we don't have lots of examples of people who look like us who have achieved success. I have experienced (as I'm sure others have as well) prejudice moments, racial tensions, decisions made based on race, or opportunities that I may have lost because of stigmas that are out there. I'm here to tell you that I did not let those obstacles stop me from achieving the level of success I'm at today. I made a conscious decision to not let those excuses bring me down or be deciding factors of what my success ceiling can be.

Rise up.

There were times when I was working at my corporate IT job when, because of how I looked or how I dressed, I was definitely put in a box of stereotypes. That I was uneducated or not leadership material. I believe that this did affect certain decisions and conversations that were had about me behind closed doors. However, I believe that we put a lot of these limiting factors in our own heads where they plot and scheme on our downfall. A lot of that is our personal mindset and our inner circles of who we speak to. I'm not saying that racism is not happening, because it is. I'm saying it is probably happening on a lower percentage than what we give credit to. You always hear, "The white man is bringing me down. I can't go into that field because I'll never get accepted because of the color of my skin. They won't take me seriously because of who I am." These are just a few of the boxes we put ourselves in.

In my life I've had to challenge this philosophy and mindset and break through it. How do I turn what I deem is an unfair advantage that others may have and even out the odds? I have looked at situations where I may have to work harder than other individuals to get into certain areas. I've turned what other people deem as a weakness or a disadvantage into an advantage. I look at the advantages I have because of the color of my skin. I am able to talk to others and be in different communities and groups that others wouldn't have access to. I have experienced multicultural ways of life and thought processes where I am no longer coming from just one angle. I have a wider perspective. I am here

to say that being Black is beautiful. Being different is beautiful. The black culture is so amazing, others attempt to replicate, imitate, and celebrate it. I use my different style and approach to my advantage by communicating with others in a way that is relatable with some swagger added to it. **One example is with my unique experiences and style I am able to sit at the table with educated tech executives and speak that lingo they understand. At the same time can come from a place that speaks for the people that are not as fortunate to be in those rooms and bring that level of personality to the conversation.**

Now, I am just speaking from my own personal experiences and what I've been able to create for my life. I know everyone's situation is different. Your challenges could be due to your age, race/ethnicity, religion, disability, gender, or more. I know you are stressed. I know you are tired. I understand it is hard to get past the history. It's hard to be fighting for the same things over and over that you feel are owed to you. When it boils down to what can you do as an individual that you can change immediately. What do you have control over? That is what you need to realize and accept. You have to see where you're at now and how you can even out those odds for more opportunities and more chances of success.

Rise up and take a step.

There are many people who look like you, sound like you, and grew up in areas like you who have made tremendous lives for themselves. I'm not talking just financially. I'm talking within their own circles and communities. Within their own families and friends. Helping the next generation just a little bit more for a better chance. I'm here to tell you that it is possible. You have to come to a conscious decision within yourself and ask yourself this question: "Am I next?"

Jamar Jones

Lessons/Takeaways

As a Black man I'm faced with a disadvantage. Putting a hood on and walking around downtown, eventually someone is going to be looking at me like I'm suspect. Unfortunately, there is nothing I can do about the view of the world and what police do or do not deem as suspicious right now.

If you're young, if you're old, whatever race you are, don't let assumptions eat you alive. Give yourself a fighting chance. How do you make that equation equal out so you have a better chance to win? Set yourself up with the mindset that you're not owed anything.

Whatever their assumptions are, don't give it to them.

Ever heard of Event + Response = Outcome? Sometimes you can't change the event but you ALWAYS can choose your response. And your response determines the outcomes.

If I go into a business meeting, these people should treat me well because I'm a highly intelligent black man. If I come in wearing a baggy sweatshirt, a chain, and baggy pants for a job interview, they'll be like, "Bro, what the heck?" There are rules and principles that require you to understand the lay of the land.

Let's talk about MLK day. Martin Luther King lived in a time when there were laws that were against him. MLK found a way to navigate through those times and move people with his words and actions. How he dressed, how he went into different rooms. He had people from all walks of life backing him. He didn't go in there demanding, "I'm a human being so I should be treated the same." Unfortunately, it was not the same. He evened out the odds by saying. "What areas can I tackle first? How can I get support on these ideas and create a movement?" The bigger the problem, the bigger the solution has to be.

Change Your Circle, Change Your Life

Just because you feel as if you're "owed" or you feel as if something should "just be" doesn't mean you'll just get it. Even after you break through the barrier, life isn't fair. And when I say fair, I mean from the individual person's fairness level.

Event + Response = Outcome. It's about looking at the playing field and calculating your moves.

Analyze your options, get more opinions and feedback, and make a better decision based on the feedback. Analyze again and attack. Then repeat.

Odds are like rolling dice. What are you going to do to heighten your chances?

Action Items

Step 1: Mindset. For ten minutes write down everything you think is unfair in your life. Rapid fire. If you don't like the color of your car, put it down. Don't have the money for a car? Write it down. Everything from "I should've had better parents" to "I don't like my car." Write it down.

Step 2: Write down the ways you can make changes to reduce the unfairness. What of those things can you take control of? Take another ten minutes to write down things you can control. Don't limit yourself with these answers. If you hate your car color, you could buy a new one. You could spray paint it. Write down every option you can take in an ideal situation.

Step 3: Ask yourself and write down what it is going to take to get there. and to do that.

Are you willing to pay the price?

Step 4: What is the priority? Spend ten more minutes to figure out what it's actually going to take to get there.

Step 5: Write down technical solutions and then rate each one from 1 to 5 about whether or not you're willing to pay that price. Prioritize your list. Now take your highest-ranking one and ask yourself, "How can I create more opportunities?" or "How can I prepare myself so that this doesn't happen again?"

Step 6: Ask yourself, how much can I increase my opportunities and how much effort do I need to put in? That is how you even out the odds.

Preparation x Opportunity = Evening out the odds. The more opportunity, the more you're able to even out the odds.

Fear is necessary but all in your mind.

Fear of rejection. Fear of not fitting in. Fear of leaving something you're used to. Fear of becoming something you don't know all the answers about yet. When is the last time you stepped out of your comfort zone? When is the last time you hung out with the circle that's not the same one you've been hanging out with for the past ten years? Are the people who you've been around the same ones who are cheering you on? Or are they bringing you down? Another great question: Are you the smartest one in your circle? It's better to be the dumbest one in the room than the smartest one providing all the answers. **Why is that? It's because when you are the smartest person around others that are not on your level you are not growing. You can help them which is good but when you need to grow those moments are not there.**

Fear comes in many forms. I can see fear in the form of the unknown, a gateway or a door that you should go through, but the gatekeeper is there and saying "You got to pass this test." Then there's instinct fear, an emotional trigger that I need to keep my guard up. I think most people don't tackle that instinctive fear the most, their biggest challenge is the gateway fear. That barrier of fear. They're at that place where the unknown is behind the door and their opportunities, hopes, and dreams are behind that door and they stop. They become paralyzed or run away when they see the fear.

They can't get the courage to open it. Or to pass whatever that life test is. Take a leap, take a job, get out of a bad relationship, move. People fear the unknown.

Jamar Jones

The fear of fitting in, the fear of acceptance, fear of rejection, the fear of "What is my life going to look like?" fear of commitment, fear of responsibility.

Let's paint the scenario.

If all of a sudden, all of our circles now involved multimillionaires with different problems than our normal problems, we'd find ourselves facing a lot of new fears. Going to their circles of people. Fear of understanding their terminology because most likely you're not going to be accustomed to it. Most of all, not fitting in. There is big risk when you're wanting to **Change your Circle**. Risk brings fear. And that fear is hard to overcome. The only way to get out of that fear is to go through it.

Fear keeps you in your comfort zone. You get around a certain group of friends and you know what jokes to tell that are going to land. You build up that comfort level. You might come from a different environment.

Someone might grow up in a different geographical location and have different experiences. that's what makes us unique. Fear of judgment is big. People will question why you're hanging with them. Fear of judgement from family, friends. Let's talk about risk. You need to weigh it. People will weigh the fear over the opportunity. They put them both on a scale and they always see that the opportunity is lower on the scale.

The unknown is too scary and there is no guarantee. The guarantee comes from within your comfort zone.

People forget that, whatever zone they are in, they got there from breaking through the barrier of fear. Kids are told no so often that they assume as adults that the answer is going to be no. So they never break out of their initial comfort zones.

They don't want to branch out.

23

Change Your Circle, Change Your Life

How I discovered and navigated through fear.

I've always had the fear. In my life, I've been in unique positions. I'm a low-key kind of a chameleon. I can blend into basically any situation. Sometimes it can be a defense until I know how to interact in a room. As I got into new circles, I had to adapt.

Growing up I was on two sides of the fence and trying to find identity. I grew up in a good home. They raised me in a loving caring way. I grew up in different environments. I was in middle-class suburbs. The tricky part was I went from different environments and cultures of people. In Muskego, Wisconsin, I was the only Black kid in school, so I adjusted to fit in. **I tried to speak their lingo that I was hearing. I tried to like things the kids where into.**

But I had to figure myself out at the same time. Unfortunately, when I moved to Muskego High School where I was the only Black kid in school, I started to develop my fear and I was experiencing anger like never before, which pushed me into different circles, or I created circles that embraced anger and fear. I didn't like the circles around me so I created my own. Some of the people around me weren't the greatest influences but they fed into the anger and fear inside me which I craved. On one side of the fence, I had a good home, family, and neighborhood. I could hop back and forth between circles of good and fear. My fear was that of acceptance and fitting in.

Especially, when I moved to different cities and had to relearn everything again. You're trying to figure out who you are and hoping people will accept and like you. The only thing I honestly took with me was the anger piece. From about 15- to 19-years old, I was a very angry individual because of the feeling of not being understood.

Thinking back, the types of people I was around weren't the people who I needed to push me forward. Home life was good. But in my mindset, I still hadn't found my place in the right circle.

I learned now that a lot of people don't even have a true circle. They're wandering from circle to circle. They may have acquaintances or "friends" but they're bouncing around looking for acceptance.

When I moved to Virginia from North Carolina, I had to relearn everything for the 3rd time. I didn't talk to anyone really. I always had my hood on and headphones sitting in the hallway. I got in fights. Just trying to fit in.

I was actively performing music and pursuing a music career at the time as well. In **2009,** I moved back to Wisconsin and started working at a financial company. It was a whole different environment. I never had that corporate environment except for maybe "Take your kid to work day." I didn't know how to act and fit in. I was saying to myself, I'm with the bigwigs now. I was still stuck in the fear of not knowing.

It boils down to self-awareness. Once you have identity and come to know yourself, that's when you gain power, and you can pick and choose your solution. Teenagers have no clue what they're doing. They have no clue. They're all trying to find identity and search. To change your circle, you need to have identity, self-awareness, and self-love. There are 3 ingredients to self-awareness. Fear, confidence and perspective. Once you master each of these you will unlock yourself awareness. Don't worry all three ingredients will be discussed in depth.

In business, acknowledge fear and strangle it.

Even as this book is being written, I still have a current fear and I just strangle it. Every time I go into a situation where I am talking with an individual about something I don't know, I am fearful. Am I going to sound stupid? Am I going to mess this up? Do I continue the conversation, cancel the meeting, retreat, or just take it and squash it? There are certain industries that I know nothing about. like supply chain manufacturing.

I went to a Supply Chain Convention in 2019 and I was a deer in the headlights. I know about video and marketing but instead there was big machinery. Everyone dressed the same in uniform. I was the only one with a hat on in the whole place. Some of the other attendees talked in a language I didn't understand. So, the question became in that moment, do I retreat or do I seize the potential? For me the benefit outweighed the fear. If I didn't know what they were saying I leaned on topics I knew I could control. That's how I led conversations to get me through the first initial convo.

I remember the first time I heard the acronym RFP (Request for Proposal). I didn't know how to interact with that so I didn't ask directly what an RFP is but asked supporting questions. **I had to act like I knew what that was but at the same time learn it. Because my reputation was on the line and I wanted to level up.** Which also plays into the chapter "Winging It."

Maybe you see a good potential person to talk to at a trade show. Then the logic hits. Rational brain hits. You ask yourself, "what are the chances they will do business with me?" So, logic is, first, how are you going to do this? How are you going to pick up your feet to go over there? Are you going to stick your hand in your pocket? How do you end it? Do you have a business card? Then fear comes in.

After you question yourself a thousand times, fear creeps in. Fear is the weight on the questions. "Oh, I can't go over there. I have no business cards. I don't know what to talk about. Maybe next time I'll do it." You give fear more weight and fear make the reason not to do something or its negative impact on you so much bigger in your mind.

When that happens to me, that's when I know it's happening. I look at fear with its devilish face. I don't care about logic and I don't care about you.

Fear and logic do not matter. You take logic and fear, and you destroy them. And then you go with intent, purpose, and your "Why?": "Why am I doing this?" You repeat your why as you go talk to the person. You wing it.

So you strangle that fear and approach the situation with intent, your why. Then you just go for it. *See "Winging It."*

Change Your Circle, Change Your Life

Lesson/Takeaways:

What sucks about fear is eventually that fear will build up and you find yourself not doing anything. Nothing. You haven't had a promotion. You haven't had a new group of friends. And all of a sudden, you're complaining about life. "I can't get out there." So, this is the cycle that you repeat. Learn from it, adjust, and then repeat. Meanwhile, self-educate so the next time that moment comes up, you can tackle it.

If you don't, if you allow those fears to add up, they will consume you eventually. Then you'll turn into one of those little, cheesin gremlins like the Cheshire cat from Alice in Wonderland. Then you're the troll behind the laptop laughing and bringing others down. Don't be a gremlin. Don't ALLOW fear to control you. Take it and strangle it!

Action Items

Go to a few places or engage people that you have been thinking about for a long time. Time to deliver what you were supposed to do before. This can be somewhere you were supposed to go but afraid to. Could be a person you haven't spoken to in a long time and never resolved a conflict. Nervous to do it? Go back to your why. It stems from pain and fear. "Embrace the Pain," "Five Pillars," and "Winging It" are the chapters you need to read before acting on these action items.

Let's say you've been in a certain job for a certain time and you don't have the confidence yet to talk to your boss or HR about a promotion. You need to talk to shepherds in your circle to understand what steps you need to take in order to ask for that promotion. One thing about fear is that it will always pass. You need to have that first step of sending the email. You need to know that this is all going to pass and, at this point, all you can do is wait for a response. You're going to run into fear regularly.

Step 1: Recognize the fear.

Step 2: Confront fear with the truth and reality.

Step 3: Strangle the fear by repeating your why and burying it.

Know it is there but you can tackle it and walk out a winner. Doing it continually will help you to be better. At the end of the day, people may have something to say but most people really admire and applaud someone who has taken a shot at it.

Especially if people sense that someone is nervous, they usually try to applaud and be supportive. You need to weigh your reasoning. When you're confronted with fear, weigh your reasoning and have a conversation with yourself about possible outcomes.

Change Your Circle, Change Your Life

Make sure you identify the value that you will get from taking the risk and tackling fear.

In the next two weeks, anytime a fear moment happens, you need to go to this chapter of the book and apply these strategies. The results will be you having less fear than you had before.

Fear is either built and strengthened or dismantled and weakened.

☼ EMBRACE THE PAIN ☼

The pain can either hurt or cure depending on how you look at it.

Embrace the pain is basically the things that happen to you; embrace it because it's a life lesson and the pain is there for you to learn from. Embrace it instead of dwelling on it. Know that these are the greatest things that can happen to you. You'll have moments when nothing good is happening for you, seems like its constantly bad, thinking your life is garbage. You have two choices: dwell on it or embrace it. It's a life lesson for you. This helps you decide which circle to go into and which to be in.

When I was pursuing my music career and I suddenly tore something in my vocal cords (full story later in the book). I could either dwell on it, challenge it, or ask, how can I learn from this and what's next for me? With all that experience I got from the ages of 15 to 27, you know I had an amazing run but it was like I learned so much from that. Now I'm able to share those experiences with people and come from a different perspective, not just from a corporate mindset. In a lot of ways, it has actually helped me. You're a bum if you let your pain define you and you DON'T want to grow from it. The key there is "not growing from it." Harsh statement, I know because there are so many levels of pain. What I mean about being a bum is even the most traumatic types of pain you can always keep an, "overcome it mentality". I don't mean instantly. But over time with patience, acceptance, and a great core circle around you, you'll be amazed at what you can become.

Everyone has their journey, and your journey is also trying to find purpose. The thing is the purpose will always change from time to time. Through time you might find out that actually it's to do something else. Your purpose may change depending on the journey you're going on. People do crazy stuff, do thirty-five years in prison and they get out and are motivational speakers. But they never would've had that experience to share unless they went through their pain. An example, is there was a pilot who was in an accident and lost his legs and he was the only survivor. So now he's a speaker. It's your journey and it's where life led you. Some people's purpose may cost different things. The cost of your purpose can be very heavy. And you can't navigate around it ; unfortunately that's just the universe guiding you. Sometimes the universe will hard correct you. Say you're going down a path and you're not supposed to be there. You'll have a hard correction.

This is a bit harsh but let's say you're a drug dealer selling drugs, not saying you are but lets pretend. One day, things don't go according to plan and you're shot rushed to the ICU. That's the universe doing a hard course correction. You weren't supposed to be there, and you didn't listen to the signs along the way.

Rocking crowds and crushing stages

When I was pursuing my music career, I thought my only purpose was to do music. To share music with the world and to have my voice be heard. To inspire and motivate people. When that's your number one goal, you go through a lot. The music industry is dirty, rough and filled with false promises from so many people. They say that the music industry is one of the hardest industries to build a business in. Even through all that I started to see a glimpse of success. I was doing it for years, built a fan base. I did about a hundred shows a year. Some crowds were only a couple people; some were hundreds to thousands. Building that audience, making connections. I thought it was all clicking. Then I'm at the precipice; really it was the peak of my music career. I was doing tours, sending some proceeds to cancer research. I performed at Relay for Life Events, and at colleges across the Midwest.

Then it happened.... I'm in Minnesota and it's my second out of three shows that weekend, I'm at University of Minnesota doing what I do best. Crowd of about 200 people. The show was going so well as me and my best friend Plex (Stephen Crofford) were rocking the stage outside.

Then all of a sudden, a huge pain goes through my throat and I'm coughing up blood. Luckily the performance was outside, so I just spit it out on the side of the stage and kept performing. I didn't know what really happened, but I knew something bad happened. I knew it was blood, I could taste it. So, I kept going. I kept performing. My voice was barely hanging on. I continued the rest of the night, sold CDs and merchandise.

I went back to the hotel and got some rest. The next day it was all swollen up. Little did I know that moment would be a huge turning point in my life. I have inflamed lymph nodes in my throat to this day. I can get surgery, but I'm weary about them being around my neck. My doctor said what if you wait a few years; it might go back to normal. I still have it today. If they make a mistake, you could lose your voice. This all happened because I didn't take care of my voice and drink tea, lemon, and honey. It was a rookie mistake that cost me everything.

I kept doing music because it was my purpose. I was deep in my IT job and excelling at that but my purpose I thought was music. When you have something ripped away like that, that's your purpose, it's earth shattering.

I was depressed for two and a half years. I didn't do anything. I was on medication for a brief time and didn't really record much music. Then I was hit with the question of do I keep making music?

I'd try, make two songs, and not be able to talk for two days. Not to mention the performances were the worst and I couldn't talk for at least four days.

I was devastated.

I could've let it destroy me.

I started to look deep within and realized that music had just been the vehicle. I just wanted to do something to change and impact the world, put my stamp on it.

I wanted to help people Through my platform, money, and connections. Music was the vehicle that I thought would get me there but unfortunately that vehicle crashed.

I had to make a choice to know my life was still meant for something great.

That's when I created my business, Foureva Productions. Through this vehicle, I'm still getting the same gratifications... just with less bums. Okay, it's not all the same, because those crowds were amazing. but my impact is on a whole other level with what I'm doing today.

Business Story

When I was working in the IT field, I had a manager who pushed me to the brink of getting fired. I will not mention her name as I'm going to take the high road here. Let's just call her Cruella for the sake of the book. She didn't like me for whatever reason. This was my new boss. I could not get any ideas across to her. She didn't want to learn what was going on our production team or the business when she started; and she didn't understand what we were doing. She would take the work and put it on us and not make changes to support the decisions she made.

She was condescending which grew my stress level to the max. I was thinking "How can I get across to this lady?" She had no real IT experience. She had no idea where we were coming from. She didn't want to hear it. She was two-faced. Like that good old song my dad sings all the time, "Backstabbers by The O'Jays" Sing it with me: "They smile in your face" Oh yea you know the rest.

I tried to get through to this woman and it wouldn't work. She was not changing. So, after months I went to the VP with my concerns about what she was doing to the organization and he brushed me off. He said learn to deal with it and it might be me who needs to learn how to work with a different management style. I was at square one once again with no one listening. It's amazing that sometimes the people who care so much for the business are the ones who suffer the most. But anyway, back to the story.

I talked to my former manager, Rick. He told me you have to learn how to deal with other types of people. He asked key questions. How else can you deal with her? What can you learn from this situation?

I took a one- or two-day training course on how to deal with and talk to difficult people. The main takeaway was I had to make them think that it was their idea. Until I made it her idea, she wanted no part of it. You have to give them all of the shine. I could have quit, got fired, kept pressing, or embrace what's happening and say what do I learn from this and how do I adjust. You have to learn how to deal with all types of people is what Rick told me.

Fast forward a few more months. I was on a flight to Atlanta for vacation and I had a surprise phone call from my former manager Rick letting me know that she was fired!

I was so happy. I got to keep my job, I learned a life lesson from it, and the witch was gone. Rick showed me what I could do. J learned more soft skills, and how to get more ideas across. It worked out at the end.

One of the worst bosses I ever had, but I was taught some of my life's greatest lessons.

Lessons/Takeaways

When pain is put into your life, first it's about understanding it and becoming one with the pain. Instead of dwelling on it, when it hits you, you react. It's about it hitting you and saying, how can I learn from this? How can I grow from this when it hits me? Physical, emotional, traumatic, death in family, are a few types of pain. You need to just be able to look it in its face and ask yourself, is this going to make or break me? Or is this a calling card that I need to come to grips with?

Someone I knew had a son who committed suicide at the age of fourteen. Now he's speaking at suicidal prevention programs, schools, and more. He's just a caring father that now he's able to help others through his unique story. He said how he looked his loss in the face and said, what am I to learn from this? He tried to see the signs and his purpose was realized through that tragedy. The lesson is, you have to look at it, learn from it, and ask, what am I supposed to learn from it? What am I supposed to do next? It could be a turning point for you, your direction, or purpose.

There are different levels of pain. It could be small pain. Example being I lost my job, or I'm always stuck in traffic. Even the small pains: Ask yourself, what are they trying to teach you?

How do you approach those situations of pain? If you're in a bad circle and a lot of pain is around you, you can choose how you react to it. Do you surrender and get sucked into it? Or do you learn, how you can get better?

If everyone in your circle is selling drugs, do you want to sell drugs, too, or do you want to do something different. It's about taking in what's happening to you and reacting from that. Self-awareness.

Don't let it be your beatdown; let it be your come up. Once again, through self-awareness, you see others' pain. The pain they try to put on you. Analyze your circle and know your circle's pain. This helps you understand what they're dealing with and if they need to stay in your circle.

Be able to recognize other people's pain, so you can understand why they are who they are.

Jamar Jones

Action Items

You can let your pain hold you back or you can let your pain propel you forward. Your pain can hold you back or it can motivate you. I am not a counselor, therapist, or professional in this space. These are my viewpoints of pain. There are pains so deep you shouldn't deal with them without the help of a therapist. Examples being military experiencing war, child abuse, or harsh divorce just to name a few.

Here are the action steps that you can take to recognize and work through pain.

Step 1 - Write down (for five minutes) the things you've experienced that have caused you trauma or pain. Jot them down in short form.

Step 2 - Determine which of those pains are holding you back the most. Rank them on a scale of 1 to 3, with 1 being the most and 3 being the least. This may be a section where truths are uncovered. Make sure you seek professional help to solve these pieces as pain can often \times be accompanied with denial.

Step 3 - Rank the impact the pain has had on your life on a scale of 1 to 3 as well. Some pain may have no benefits. Be honest with yourself and list ways this pain has taught you something or been beneficial.

You discover the benefit of your pain and then you make it into motivation. Now you have a why. You might have a superpower and you might have unlocked a "why".

Your "why" can come from pain. Some pain can cut so deep it breaks you and you might need someone else to help put you back together again.

The key is, if you address and embrace your pain before a breaking point, it could make you stronger.

Your non-negotiables are your foundation

Let me line up the five pillars. In order to change your circle and change your life, you have to build self-awareness. If you're not aware of what you want, you won't know where to go or start. If you want to get anywhere, you need your foundation set. I say 5 because I feel like that's enough for a foundation and it's not selfish. What I call the 5 pillars are your 5 non-negotiables when you're trying to do something whether in business, in relationships, with friends, with family, or concerning your health mental. What are the five values you refuse to compromise?

For example, you've always made 25k in business and your non-negotiable is, "I need to make 50k/year." That takes away a lot of other things that you don't need to mess with anymore or even think about like certain jobs that are available, skill level, or industries.

Another would be, "I need a career where I can teach people." So maybe I can work in the area of management, mentoring or coaching.

A third pillar might be "flexible income." Maybe you want multiple streams of income so that you are not dependent on one. You move out all of the noise and you get clear about what you want.

My divorce that unlocked my self-awareness

I went through a heartbreaking divorce. Through that experience, I learned about self-awareness. And through that self-awareness I learned about the five pillars. While I was still in that relationship, I had to figure out what I wanted in a relationship, especially with someone I had been with since high school. Ten years plus and I had never really thought about what my relationship pillars would be.

40

Jamar Jones

A lot of people get in relationships and don't think about what they want. Next thing you know, you fall in love, have kids, and you're caught in a cycle. Then years later you may be asking "why aren't we talking?" For most people it starts that there's a rollercoaster of physical fun and fresh new excitement. After a while, you're just kind of riding the rollercoaster and forget why you got on it in the first place. You have to be synched in on different levels and you have to think about what you want.

When all of this happened to me, I had to reevaluate. Especially after a divorce, you have to re-evaluate. You ask, why did I go through with it? It wasn't hate for me, I just knew over twelve years of my life had already been spent on this relationship. Do I want to give another twelve years when these five pillars aren't being met?

Because you're questioning all the things you like and don't like but then it comes to what do you actually want? So, let's say I'm single again, what am I looking for? Why could this situation not work? But if you don't have your pillars set, you're setting yourself and your partner up for failure.

I wrote down all of the things I wanted on a big board/wish list. Then I started to put them in sections. I have literally a piece of paper with these. One is intellectual. I want someone I can have an intellectual relationship with. I want to talk about my ideas, goals, dreams and so much more. I wanted someone who I could grow with. If I'm asking challenging questions, I would want the same challenging questions in the return. You make your own pillars. These pillars are the foundation holding up everything else. She would be one that I could talk to and would be supportive. I was looking for the next step further of challenging me to grow as an individual.

Another aspect is I need someone who loves themselves as they need to be one with themselves before they can love anyone else. Self-love is most times a hard lesson to learn but so necessary to love someone else. When you love and understand yourself you can effectively love someone else with all your heart intentionally. You're not dependent on that person. That person doesn't make you whole. They elevate you. Through my relationship I tried to share self-love and wait for her to recognize it truly within herself. She made leaps and bounds over the 12 years, but she still was depending on me for happiness. In a strange way, I thought the divorce would force her to see the change that needed to be made and unlock her dreams, aspirations, and self-worth. I do think she learned a lot but even a few years later after the divorce it still looks like she hasn't cracked the code yet. I hope I'm wrong because I truly want the best for her and hoping one day she looks beneath the surface and finds true self love.

These pillars gave me the clarity to know that I was in the wrong relationship. Even though I loved this person, cared for this person, wanted the best for this person. But for me, she wasn't who I needed to elevate me and rise to my life purpose. Twelve years was enough time. The key is if you know the change you want will never happen, but I hope so...that's the time you should know it's never going to change. But people will change on their own time.

You leaving might be the trigger for them to change. I felt like I was constantly trying to change someone, and I didn't want to be in this position. I know my pillars now. I hope they did the same thing for themselves and I wish them nothing but the best.

Lessons/Takeaways

Pillars are your only compass. I'd say go through all of your wants, put them onto a non-negotiable checklist of things that you need, and do a re-check annually. Some you don't need to re-evaluate like intellectual, self-love for example; but re-evaluate health for example. Change as circumstances change so you need to re-evaluate them. In my situation, I wouldn't have known where to go next or what direction I was already going, or if I was growing as an individual. If you want to know where to go, you have to have the five pillars. They are your non-negotiable foundation for your life. They are the structure that's holding everything up for you.

People need to do it in all areas but especially in relationships, with all other people, and in business for sure. When I got downsized, I definitely thought about everything. Do I get another job? Do I do my own thing? What do I do? I wrote down "What am I after?" and "What am I trying to accomplish?" I've always wanted to build and create something. I wrote down everything I was good at, who I knew right now, and that I wanted to build something that was my own. What does that look like? That's when I started crafting around "I'm good at these things; I can offer them as a service." But as I grew in business, many aspects of that changed. Non-negotiables became clearer.

Having your own pillars for your circle will help you understand who needs to be in it. Once you set goals and determine your wants, you'll see who is in your circle who shouldn't be and who isn't in your circle who should be. Now you have direction. You both make a list (partners) of your pillars, if after the convo the conversation is had does this person that need to be in your life anymore. You have to make a choice. Will the person change? Don't wait and don't change. By doing the pillars you learn how to love yourself more. You're now not taking the time to do everything else? When is it your time and when are you growing?

Change Your Circle, Change Your Life

You have to see it on paper, and you write it out. You'll realize that nothing here is lining up and you've neglected this for so long. You ask, how long have I neglected this? If you don't ever take the time to acknowledge it, you're never going to find the time to love yourself, to care about the stuff you have going on. What about you? Everyone is so concerned, and your life is messed up.

Action Items

Move out all of the noise and get clear about what you want.

Step 1: Go into all your wants and put them into non-negotiable things that you want to do once a year. You can put them in different "buckets": relationships, career, etc. List your wants in every category. What do you want in a relationship? What do you want from your friends?

Step 2: Pick 5 core non-negotiables for each pillar and write them down. These you need to re-evaluate annually as circumstances may change.

Step 3: Look at each non-negotiable within each pillar. How do they align, for instance, with your professional career circle? In what areas are you not meeting your non-negotiables? Let's say your non-negotiable is you want to make 100k/year. Match up your current situation and current circle with your non-negotiables.

Step 4: Make one step to align with your non-negotiables. Have a conversation with your boss, or with your partner, or with yourself to determine if you're spending enough time on yourself and your health. Write down one step you can take for each of these.

Now you have your 5 pillars written out and your non-negotiables on each pillar. Continue that until you've reached all of your actions for each of your 5 pillars. 5 pillars and 5 non-negotiables within each pillar. When you're done with this exercise and have your foundation, determine if anything new (new relationship, new diet) has filtered in through your non-negotiables. Anything new needs to go through the process as well so nothing slips through the cracks.

Learning is a powerful tool but don't forget the Swag

Education is vital for how you move on the chessboard of life. Book smarts and street smarts: You need both types of education to move from circle to circle.

The more education you have, the higher probability that it will actually pan out to something good. When you have zero education, for example, at a construction site you wouldn't know what to do, or what is going on. This is where the street smarts come in. It's kind of a pulley system. If you have good soft skills and can navigate multiple personalities, you can communicate with all people. You can start to click with personalities and be able to get your foot in the door. You're able to compete. You can weasel your way in but you have to then put in work. At the end of the day, there are two things to work at. Book smarts and street smarts have to work together in balance. If you can keep your pulley system balanced, that's better than having one or the other extreme. You can be accepted even if you don't know all of the technical/book smart pieces of it. Eventually, though, you'll have to deliver.

The saying, "It's not what you know; it's who you know" is true until you have to perform and deliver. You can secret agent your way in but then you have to deliver. I can infiltrate but then it's like the Mandalorian TV show on streaming platform that has an episode when they infiltrate a base of the enemy and right as they were about to get access a enemy guard asks them, "What's the code"? And they didn't know the number. (They were pretending to blend in.) At some point you need to deliver for the validation.

In this chapter I focus on the difference between street and book smart, and on self-education and continued education. I begin by expanding on the idea of having a flexible title.

If you want to get somewhere in life, you're going to have to flex your title. I know in society, especially when I was in middle school or high school, and they asked, "What do you want to be?" they had you pick your identity/title and then you went to school for a long time striving to attain that title. People hyper focus on this title.

The thing about a title is, you can have a goal of what you want to achieve. "I want to become an author. I want to be a well-respected dentist." If it's a headline, shoot for that. But don't shoot for that to be your only thing. Even if it's a lawyer or attorney, don't shoot for the title; shoot for the goal. Difference is a goal may be to help injustice in the system, so people are represented correctly. There's a lot of ways you can go about that. A title puts you in a box of just that position.

Your title will fluctuate as you grow through life. depending on your circles and your evolving goals. My title has changed many times over the years. You need to know that your title is not what defines you; you need to focus on your goal.

It's like the saying, "when people are wearing many hats." For instance, say your goal is to be an IT manager with a company. You decide that's your goal and tell yourself, "That's what I'm going to school for." You find a job whose title is IT manager.

Next thing you know, you got to talk to your boss but they want to go somewhere after work to play golf You need to learn a little bit about golf to connect with them. Even as your friend circle changes, your title might change from IT manager to golfer.

You are always going to be a student of life.

You can become an expert in certain areas of life, but you're never going to figure it all out. You have to think, "I have to be a student/ I have to continue to learn." That mindset will help you to not be disappointed when things don't go your way. You'll have more of a problem-solving mindset. Can't get a job? Might have to become a student of learning more about the interview process. You went to school and got the piece of paper. Now you have to get the job.

Education is expensive.

It's pricey. You pay in your time (learning new things) and you pay in failure (how could you adjust and do things differently). Your failure is really a learning opportunity because of your lack of education. You had to learn and that's the price you pay. Are you willing to pay the price for college, for courses, for certification, for textbooks? You pay in not only money but sanity, mental health, break-ups. You are now learning about different things and it could cost you the loss of relationships and heartache. If you want to fast track your education, see **"Find a Mentor."**

Learn from others' failures. Sometimes you have to put that bread up or you can pay with time.

How can you shadow someone for that education? Learn the ins and outs. Talk with multiple people in the area you want to be in.

People are realizing how much they can do with self-education. The internet has exploded with online seminars and workshops. I feel like not following the traditional, conventional methods still carries a stigma that places you at a disadvantage against someone who has followed the traditional path. However, I feel like my non-traditional/self-education route has actually prepared and educated me better than someone who went through the traditional route. You're limited by the system and, for instance, the people who have taught you. That's what's cool about self-education. I can choose which system works for me. Do I want to learn at a retreat, through an in-person tutor, or via group education? There are so many ways to self-educate outside the classroom.

Jamar Jones

I have zero formal education on video production. I am completely self-taught. I would challenge anyone who has been through formal/traditional methods and they won't know a quarter of the video production I now know. I'm constantly self-educating but also, I'm getting personal experience in my field. On the other hand, the experience level of students who come out of the traditional methods is low.

Imagine there is a pulley system and going through school the traditional way is a baseline. Then comes further and continued education. Experience takes it further. I believe that if you rate both forms of education for yourself (talking about traditional and self-education), self-education needs to be so much higher. It weighs more than a traditional education. If it doesn't, you now know what you need to do.

If you're chasing job titles for your career path, you're actually less valuable than someone who is chasing goals.

If someone wants to be a really good leader, they're going to learn from multiple areas. They're focused on being a great leader, not being the CMO of a company. What happens when people chase titles is, they get promoted to C-Suite level positions that they aren't prepared for at all.

Street smarts: That's how you move. If you don't have street smarts, you can't move the way you want to. The street smarts are a combination of your instincts, your ability to observe, and your ability to communicate and talk with people. You can develop street smarts by building on your self-awareness and your ability to communicate with others. If you're book smart, your circle of opportunity is limited by resume and chance. Book smarts are like your brain, your mind. They're the stuff you hold onto, your own internal bank of knowledge. With street smarts, your range of opportunities is way bigger.

Street smarts are the vehicle to where you want to go. Book smarts are the delivery.

Failures equals Success

Before opening Foureva Media, I was working for a financial company named PLS. While I was there, my education was frequently questioned. In "Embrace the Pain," I told you the full story about my old boss, Cruella and my experience with the company. I had learned about the price of education because it almost cost me my job.

I was in a bad situation where Cruella, would not hear me out on anything. It was a constant battle to be heard. I felt as if she was trying to catch me messing up instead of helping me grow.

Through that experience, I was forced to educating myself about how to deal with that type of person. If this would've never come up, I probably wouldn't have looked up how to deal with difficult people. Life gave me a test and I had to see if I could pass it. Luckily, I had people in my circle saying, "Okay, you're presented with this problem. What can you do about it?" I took a course that provided me with tactics. Now whenever this situation comes up, I am prepared.

The more self-education you have, the greater your competitive advantage. The less education you have (street or book smart), the greater your disadvantage. Now looking back from that moment, I realize it made me smarter in similar situations. I now know how to deal with difficult people because my self-education taught me that.

Preparation is vital to execution

If I don't know something, I turn into a bookworm searching for information. There was an education videography project that I shot with another videographer. As we talked through the shoot, it sounded like something I could handle. The problem was, I had never shot an actual training course before. Kids attending the training created another obstacle as far as shooting the video. I didn't have equipment properly charged, I didn't have my mics charged, and I didn't do all the proper research on the project. I also didn't film all the right angles for an educational program. It was a multi-day shoot.

After the shoot when I watched the footage, I was able to see everything I did not do correctly. Everything was captured in high-quality video image but the way it was framed, the audio. and the structure of it wasn't organized very well.

Looking back, I believe this is more than likely the reason why they never got back to me for additional projects and work. I entered too unprepared, and they could sense that I didn't fully know how to structure a training program. I didn't segment it out like I should have. If I had done more pre-production planning and self-education, perhaps they would've gotten back to me. This company did let me know they were going to do a lot more of these videos and I know that they probably didn't want me working on them.

This story doesn't have a happy ending, but it has a lesson: Prepare for opportunities as much as possible. The more you can, the better the results. Looking back, I should have prepared more and asked some other videographers how they would go about this educational video with kids. Then I could have avoided some of the missteps along the way. The best thing I did was I took on the challenge and did not pass on the project. I learned so much from this experience and if I had passed on it I would have learned nothing.

"By failing to prepare, you are preparing to fail."

Change Your Circle, Change Your Life

Lessons/Takeaway

Look at your circle and identify who has the right vehicle that you can get into to reach your goals. Are they going places? How often are they going? Then look at that same circle and ask how many people can actually deliver on what they say they can do. They're a lot of people out there who can talk a good game, weasel or wing their way in. They tell you it's coming soon. It's on the way.

But when it's time to deliver an actual result or an action, they can't do it. They're nowhere to be found.

Because I combine street smarts with book smarts and self-learning, I'm able to do a lot more than most people.

Security...if you want real job security, relationship security, to even out the odds, family security, living security, then you need to continue to self-educate. You need to surround yourself with people who are going where you want to be. You need to learn it because it's literally free. For absolutely anything. Besides that, there are a lot of self-help books, audios, and other training tools. A lot are free but if you want to pay, you can do that as well.

There are a lot of organizations, associations, events, and community leaders who are doing things that you might want to learn. You can apply this to all aspects of life. Do you want to learn about fitness, about Keto, about bettering your health? It's out there for free and there are groups and events of people who are in that space. Search on social media, local magazines, or school organizations just to name a few. Evaluate the group by activity of members and see if it is a good fit for you.

You need to self-educate continuously and often. The more you can educate yourself, the more you're going to fast track your situation. The more you can do, the faster you can go. Think about that in every aspect of your life. Because that can determine where you end up and where everyone else in your life ends up as well.

Jamar Jones

I am not a programmer. I am not a developer. But if I wanted to get started to be one, here's how I'd go about it. First, I'd find social media groups or social communities and start interacting in those groups.

I'd ask questions, pick their brains, get feedback. I'd watch as many free videos on coding as I could.

I'd figure out what computer to use, what kinds of code I need to learn. what tools I need to purchase.

I'd then look online and see if there were any local meetups where I could converse with others on this topic. I'd find an association or organization that I could potentially do some free work for—a small website, for instance.

Doing this helps me build my portfolio, my confidence, and my experience while helping me fulfill my purpose. Someone is now expecting something from me. It's like homework. If your teacher were to give you a test in college, you would have to learn the material and turn in your assignment at a certain time.

The free opportunities that you can drum up for a friend or an organization.

Those are now your teachers at the school. They're waiting for your homework. What is the assignment? What is the communication like? That's your feedback. You essentially just took yourself to school.

These are just some initial first steps I'd take to becoming a developer or programmer.

Essentially, when you're doing this type of work for free, it's not free. You're paying for the experience and the time. When you start to build a portfolio of your work, you're now getting that piece of paper from the school. You're getting your degree. You have something to show people. In this day and age, a portfolio looks way better than a degree. If you can have both, you're even more dangerous!

Change Your Circle, Change Your Life

Action Items

I want to reference ways that people can sharpen each skill sets but, again, this mindset is more about self-education than formal education. It's about the pursuit of learning and figuring things out for the experience. Always keep building your personal development. The education and experience that you have are what get you through the door. When review time comes, it's not always about technical skills. The soft skills are usually how you climb.

Step 1 - Spend five minutes writing down all of the things you'd like to do, titles you'd like to obtain, or how'd you'd ideally like to be described, titled, and perceived. What headlines do you want to be associated with your name? What occupation? What future desires? Manager, parent, woodworker, football coach, author, activist, outdoorsman.

Step 2 - Write down your strengths and weaknesses as a person. Be honest with yourself. I'm not very organized, I'm great at public speaking, I'm punctual but struggle with long conversations. These should be soft skills that are strengths and weaknesses.

Step 3: Start to research. Say you wrote down that you'd like to be a pilot for step 2. Start researching what it is like to be a pilot and what it takes to become one. Make sure you are doing your best to always use credible, factual sources.

Your main goal is to obtain both types of education: formal schooling and informal/street smarts. You need to always be hungry for more information. Know that you will always need to continue to learn no matter what. You need to have a constant pursuit of knowledge and education. What things are you already good at? What do you think about the new things you've learned in the past year? It could be anything from learning about new wines to learning how to change a tire on your car. Things that stand out that you've learned in the past year. If you have nothing to write down in your soft skills, you need to think about what actionable steps you can take in order to educate yourself to achieve your goals. What are your current titles and what do you want to be true about them in a year? Who do you want to be and what do you want to learn?

Step 4 - Self-Assess: Write down new things you've learned in the past year. Put everything into two categories: mindset (knowledge) and technical (physical activities). Next, write down what you'd like to learn in each category. In the next thirty days, educate and research in order to achieve or work towards these goals. Spend at least ten to twenty percent of your time learning. You looked at what you did last year to see your current state. Write down two mindset goals and two technical goals that you'd like to achieve.

Step 5: Get to work on your goals! Start by thinking about any free time in your day when you could begin to implement this learning. Drive while listening to a podcast. Get ready in the morning and put on an audio book. You can learn new things while working out, over lunch breaks, on your way to work/traveling, during bathroom breaks, or waiting in line at the supermarket. Here are a few ways you can educate yourself: podcasts, social media pages, documentaries/tv shows, YouTube and other videos, Masterclass, TED talks, Udemy, online courses, seminars or life events, virtual events, join a group or club, shadow someone, ask your employer, networking, library/books, join a class, find a mentor (see "Find a Mentor"}. Choose at least three ways that you'd like to learn. Every single day make sure that you're staying consistent and learning. Hold yourself accountable.

• If you've set your goals and you've read chapter "Go for the Championship" feel free to align what you're doing here with those goals.

WINGING IT

Confidence can weather any Storm

Winging it has been a philosophy of mine for a long time: going into a situation that you're not fully prepared for and knowing that you have the confidence to succeed in it. I go into situations where I may not be prepared or have a strategic plan, but I have my philosophy of "Perfection is what kills you and kills growth."

I prepare to a certain extent, but I also wing it and find a way to deliver. Or going into a situation wondering if I'm 100% qualified that I have the confidence to figure it out.

Not over preparing or letting perfection stunt your opportunities. To be honest you can wing it all your life, but it will bite you on the backside if you're not quick on your feet or you don't have an agile thought process.

You also have to wing it in the right opportunities. You can wing it in all aspects of life but some you shouldn't. For example, not a marriage or a tattoo. If you get super nervous talking to someone, just go and try it out with confidence. You're rising to the occasion. You don't always have to be 100% prepared to take on a task or opportunity.

You don't fully know the scope of everything you need to talk about; you didn't do all of the background research. But you have enough confidence that you'll rise to the occasion. You put it on yourself that you can excel. This trait is needed to succeed. If you're a full perfectionist, nothing is ever going to get done. To get into those other circles you're not necessarily going to know before you get in there. You have to have the confidence and willingness to be vulnerable. Say I wanted to do Tae Kwan Do. I don't know the background or speak the language so I'm not going to take the first step.

You have to have the confidence within yourself to talk to people, do some small talk, and be willing to learn and soak it in at that point in time. You're not always going to have everything lined up. If I was teaching someone how to wing it, I would say to power study whatever you can. Whatever you are trying to get involved in, learn as much as you can and as your learning use your confidence to get involved. Take it in steps and apply your new found learnings to your current situations that you are creating.

Dive into it. Dive into whatever that topic or area is if you have time before you wing it.

If you're called up to the room at the drop of a hat, know your confidence and tap into what you have. That gives you a boost before you go into the wolves' den. Talking about the audience here. If you have really good people/soft skills, you're winging it skills will always excel over a bookworm approach.

Emotional Intelligence: The actual definition is "the capacity to be aware of, control, and express one's emotions, and to handle interpersonal relationships judiciously and empathetically."

You're able to adapt and feed off it. You have to try to be relatable as much as you can. You have to gauge when the right time to wing it is. For me, eight times out of ten, I'm winging it over missing the opportunity. Period. I recommend getting a book or two on emotional intelligence. This will help so much with the understanding and how deep this goes.

Winging it made me who I am Today

For sure PLS is an example of me winging it. To be a manager of a team, reporting to a team wasn't the issue, it was reporting to your boss and then interacting with other departments in the company.

The hardest part was when I had to deliver reports on how or why I do things to upper management. Especially when their track record made it look like they had it all together. I'm trying to come in there and tell them how to do something. It's difficult to do that when you are still learning yourself.

For instance, when we had to sell ideas to infrastructure and we had to talk about systems, networking, and security, areas where we might not know the terminology. All we knew was we needed to sell this to them to try to change or adjust these situations to help our department. You had to truly wing it and it was tough. There were times I had to give presentations to groups of higher ups, from director to C-Suite Level people.

I remember a time that I had to go to Chicago to the corporate office. Our office was located in Brookfield, WI. I had to give a presentation to a few C-Suite level executives and one of the presidents of the company. PLS had a beautiful high rising office that overlooked downtown Chicago. I feel like the more stunning the office the more your blood pressure goes up in the room. When I walked in and begin my presentation that I prepared their became moments that I wasn't fully ready for. The room started to ask questions looking for more insight. Topics comes up and I didn't to miss out on the moment. I had to rise up to the occasion and try to articulate it the best way I could. The best tools that got me through those moments were the soft skills, not the technical skills. I ended up knocking out that presentation and they were sold on the ideas and loved the direction the team was going.

One trick that works in those moments is in layman terms, help people get on board without having to decode everything. Whenever I had to talk to district managers or directors of operations, I had to do actual presentations in front of everyone. When I had to do it alone, there were moments I knew exactly what I was talking about and then there were other times when it would get down to like store-level technical matters where I had to wing it. I rose to the occasion and showed up. At times I dropped the ball and stuttered my way through.

I remember I apologized to Rick Hartline, my former manager at

Jamar Jones

PLS on the train on the way home from the presentation and he said it was okay. I failed in the micro of it but I showed up for the moment. You have to show up and wing it in the moment. Pretty much my entire life, I've gotten into things I'm technically not qualified for. PLS and opening my own business are two. I'm a people person and I'm a book worm. When I need to learn something, I deep dive into what I need to learn. I learn as I go.

When I started my Foureva Productions Videography and Photography business, I had a camera, but I had no idea how to use it. Then I booked my first music video. Funny, right?!

I knew the idea of a music video and was using a kit lens. I look back and cringe. After that I went into learning more about equipment and diving deeper. Through the opportunities, on the back end I'm learning. When an opportunity shows up, I wing it and figure it out as we go.

The first big event was a bodybuilder competition that I had the opportunity to do and here's the thing, I knew nothing about taking body building videos and photos. I worked out a deal where we would charge a lot less than a typical videography company. So, I had to get together a team and I didn't have the experience for that either. But I used to manage a team in my IT job, so I took that experience to help me through.

Throughout my time, I approached different opportunities and I completely winged it. The body building event, I completely winged it and they invited me again. Now, fast forward, we do big events, large conferences, and trade show events and execute at a high level. I learned a lot through doing the body building event. I upped the game by going back, assessing what we could do next time, learning from others in the same field, then adjusting and executing on the next one. I built a whole company on that. The philosophy can be used as almost everything. I was lucky enough to film a TV show pilot with a Hollywood producer who filmed *The Wire*. I did that not knowing about what goes into a TV show. I just learned, adapted, and took the opportunity. When I'm around people who know stuff and I don't know as much, I'm a sponge. When you're not the smartest person in the circle, you're in the right circle.

Personal Circles and Conversation

I'm not into pop culture so I don't know a ton of TV show actors or references. But I can generally make myself feel at home in a room. I just ask questions and look to learn more than to act like I have the answers. I know a lot of people can relate to situations like this.

For example, family get-togethers back in the day with my ex. A lot of times I had to keep my composure and blend in. I was trying to mold my way in there to be accepted by the family, so I winged it at every family get-together. A lot of her family were country minded. So, I didn't understand a lot of their references

I had to ask questions and wing it. Sometimes you don't need the answer if you show confidence and have the right poise in the room.

Jamar Jones

Lessons/Takeaways

Wherever you need to go in your life, you will need to learn the art form of winging it. You will never be 100% prepared or qualified for every opportunity that is presented to you.

That will make or break the direction you're going in. This goes for everything. Example: You just got a promotion. You're now a manager and you've never done it before, and you have to learn quickly or you're going to sink. You have to learn how to do it and apply your confidence as you go.

I've been able to progress so fast by winging it. Get the feedback after. Then ask what do I need to change or adjust to tackle the next opportunity. A lot of people will get comfortable in their one spot. When the opportunity comes up to advance, they pass on it and remain in the same job. They're not growing as individuals. Some people don't like the change. They have fear in them and retreat to what they already know.

Unfortunately for any human being, you have to face fear to grow as a person. Being comfortable at some point you're going to lose. Even if you are doing something you love but you are comfortable, you should continue challenge yourself and push yourself out of the comfort zone. You get so comfortable you don't want to try a new opportunity or relationship. What's going to happen is eventually it'll catch up to you. You work the same job every year for thirty years. You stop exercising your mind and your talent. Then the company goes under. What are you going to do? Who is going to hire you? You've done the same thing for thirty years.

That happiness level of comfort is the devil. You have to be able to get out there and try new things. Know that comfort is death. The moment you get comfortable, you're losing. You're doing yourself a disservice. You're comfortable in a relationship for a while and you're thinking everything is good. You're used to the same old same old. Eventually something will crack or happen. It will boil up if you're not keeping it fresh. Humans need to grow and evolve, refresh. They're not supposed to wither away in a corner somewhere.

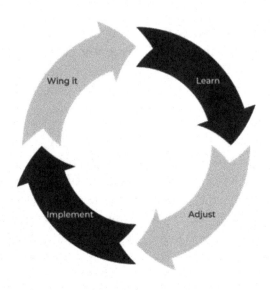

Action Items

Step 1: Jot down four areas that you want to get into and then find circles or paths to that area. They need to challenge themselves and within the next two weeks you need to get yourself into these circles and just go for it. Go to a networking event or a class. Show up and wing it!

Step 2: Identify four new circles that you want to get into. Do an hour of prep for each circle and find a path to interact with that circle. Examples: Join a Facebook group and talk to the organizer. Talk to your current circle and ask who they know. Go to a seminar or training or a class. Find a way to get into these spots and insert yourself. Show up if you don't know anything about it. Do fifteen minutes of research on each of the four circles and in about one hour you're able to change your life. Start winging it.

Step 3: Confidence comes from doing. Put yourself in more situations where you can deliver. Say yes to every opportunity dealing with those four areas that you've identified.

Step 4: For each area, post on social media that you're doing these things. Tell your immediate circle what you're doing and what these four areas are. In this way, you're outwardly letting everyone know you're doing this. Then ask, "Do you know anyone in these industries as I'd like to get something started to learn about this field?"

Step 5: Go into four circles and pick one business and one personal connection. Pick one comfort zone you're not confident in that you want to get into. This could be a personal or business goal. Then determine four different circles that are targeting this goal. Maybe a Facebook group is one circle. Maybe a networking group is another circle. Perhaps an event or a place that sells a commodity. Go speak to a manager.

Step 6: Pick out the circle and then take fifteen minutes to research it before you have contact. I want you to post at least eight times in the next two weeks that you're doing this. You need to advertise you're in this space. The next two weeks, you're telling everyone what you're doing through posts. Lastly, when you're in these circles, your offer is not to accept money.

Create interactions for free. Anytime you introduce money as a barrier, people might say no. Say yes for no money. You want to get into this new area. You are getting paid in experience.

Once again, education is expensive. You're getting paid in experience. What's more important than the money? Confidence and a portfolio.

FIND A MENTOR

A guide in life is like a cheat code in a video game.

The reason you need a mentor is because life doesn't have a written path for you to go on and it doesn't have instructions or a rule book.

When you're trying to figure out your life journey and what circles to be in, you're going to need guidance. Do you want to know the truth? The truth is you're always going to need someone else to get you where you need to go. It's *impossible* to do alone. You're going to need someone else to get you to the next level or platform.

You need a mentor to help guide you to where you need to go. Even if you invent something amazing by yourself, to get it out there in the world...in order to sell, patent it, or to fast track it, you need a mentor.

A mentor

1. Is someone who believes in you. They have to see it in you, even when you don't see it in yourself.

2. Has to be somewhat in the field that you're striving to enter.

3. Needs to push your limits by constantly testing you.

I few mentors I can name for myself are my dad Mayo Jones, my mom Allison Jones, Cristina Ferreira, Keith Coleman, Rick Hartline, my Uncle Lamont, and Grandpa. I had a high school teacher I looked up to at one point in my life as well, Mr. Bosch. You need a mentor for each path. There is a difference between a role model and a mentor. A role model is someone who you view as someone you can model your life after and see yourself in. A mentor is someone who personally affects your life for the better and intentionally builds your growth.

Change Your Circle, Change Your Life

My first mentor in business is who I call the God Father, Rick Hartline.

Rick Hartline was my manager at my IT job at PLS. What's interesting about him is he gave me a shot when I had no business being given a shot. Actually, Randy Wilinski, a good friend of mine and coworker, paved the way for Rick's mindset to change what is possible and reopened his mind on ways to reorganize an organization. Randy came in with no experience, owned it, and outperformed everyone. It opened his mind up to the fact that "Maybe I can just repeat this and built people up." That's where I stumbled in. I was working at Menards when I got a call from my ex-best friend's mom that her work was hiring for support positions and you didn't need any experience.

I wasn't getting enough hours in at Menards, so I took her up on her offer.

I walked in with a backwards hat, just my normal everyday clothes, to see the office. I talked with Rick for a brief moment and left not really knowing what to expect. I had no real interview.

I knew someone who vouched for me to get in the door.

I called him up a week later and I asked, "Do I have the job?" He said, "Yeah, come in tomorrow."

And that's how it all started. It even took a while to get me all setup in the system, that shows you how off the cuff this was. Rick gave me a shot as someone else had paved the way. He started as a boss and transformed into a mentor. Meanwhile, I was pursuing my music career on the side. I did that for two years and it was way more important than my IT job. My mindset was the job just paid the bills. I'm clocking in and I'm clocking out.

At the time, our department was small and didn't have all the right structure in place. We had no leader really because Rick was doing a lot of roles in the company and his concern was about everything else that happened with the business. He wasn't hyper focused on the support department. They eventually put Randy as team lead to add some structure.

So fast forward two years and what happens is very interesting. Something shifted in my brain because Randy was giving me more responsibilities as I was performing tasks well. He started to give me a higher level of expectation like we're counting on you to get this done. That transitioned my brain to "What I'm doing here matters." That was the shift. Then Randy gave me managerial responsibilities. Rick was supportive of those moves. Randy had to go to bat for me as these positions were made up as we went along. They were created because of what we were doing.

If we would've slacked off, the positions would've never been created. So then Rick started to see something in me. I don't know what it was. But he just said he saw kind of that fire and ambition, just within me to give me more opportunity.

Because there were several occasions where I should've been fired. I was nonchalance about the job and this was apparent at times. But he kept me on and then gave me these opportunities to rise to the occasion. I kept working and honing my skills providing value to the company. Then when Randy left the company, I was put into team lead management position. By the time this happened, I was really taking the job seriously. Then Rick sat me down and taught me about things that unlocked my brain.

He started by teaching me people skills through his training budget. He taught me how to talk to people, how to influence people, negotiation skills, and sales skills because I was just running into roadblocks at PLS. I'm trying to sell ideas and no one cares. He taught me how to move in a room. He said if you want to achieve your goals this is what you must do.

That paved the road for me, which helped my music side, my marketing side, and even growing a business to this day.

Change Your Circle, Change Your Life

There are people who help other people mold businesses. I see Rick as at the helm of it, at least training, teaching, and guiding how to go through all of it. I just started to learn all of these things and I opened my mind. It's like my mind had evolved. It just expanded and I realized there was way more. The whole time at PLS, I could always ask him questions, always go to him, confide in him no matter what was going on. He would always understand and listen. He would never judge me. Never.

There were times I was in a meeting and I'd tell him I needed to take off work because I had stuff going on. And he was like, "Look. we'll make it work. Take the time off." He was supportive of the other dreams I had and that really makes you switch your mindset. I had this thing in my mind about bigwigs all being money-hungry pigs who didn't care about people. But that was my first real job. Lucky enough, I had a good mentor who led me and formed the person I am today.

That instance was so pivotal, I wouldn't be able to run the business I'm running now without it. There's no way. A lot of business owners don't have those skills and they're capped on their potential. I'm not saying I've mastered those soft skills, but I've studied them. Like martial arts. From listening to people, I've learned persuasion, how to deal with difficult people, understanding personality traits, what makes people tick, and much more

I owe all of these skills to my mentor.

And to relate this to the circle part of the book, I had no one in my circle like this before PLS. I was messing with people who weren't as ambitious and knowledgeable. They were not talking about anything like what Rick or Randy were talking about.

Get the right people on the bus. Just like the circle. Once I got into that new circle, everything changed. Just being in an environment with those people. Funny thing, at PLS there were still circles you had to weed out. People were negative. They complained. They didn't care. Luckily, I attached myself to people like Randy Wilinski, Rick Hartline, Cory Kroll, and Carlos Caraballo.

Their mindset was completely different and that changed my whole shift. It would've never happened if I hadn't branched out and allowed my brain to evolve.

My Parents that I appreciate so much

My mom and dad have always been mentors in my life. Even when I didn't know it. Back when I was in high school, we were living in multiple places. First was Wauwatosa, Wisconsin. Then we moved to Muskego, Wisconsin then Charlotte, North Carolina. After that, we moved to Stevens City, Virginia. We did that because of layoffs and my dad had to provide for the family by any means necessary. Through that time period, I was going through a lot of change within myself and dealing with advanced anger issues as well as racial issues that came from Muskego. Looking back, I now realize that I was being helped by a lot of self-discovery during this time frame. With my parents teaching me valuable life lessons back then, I didn't even realize how impactful they were until later on in life. The level of patience my parents had to have with me during this transitional period was absolutely extraordinary. This patience taught me later on in life how to deal with extreme situations about loved ones and people closest to you.

What's interesting is that my mom and dad are very different in their approaches and the way that they deal with situations. However, their values and principles are the same. My dad is very analytical and loves to have deep conversations to discover a problem or issue. He is very caring and thorough. He is also more averse to taking risks. My mom is more free-spirited and outgoing, more of a risk taker, and very compassionate but she does not mess around. (she'll like that line). She sees the world more for living for the now while my dad is a planner and a strategic person who watches every step he takes. This balance of two personalities that I grew up with taught me both sides of the coin. One thing is for certain: My parents always gave me an open door to talk with them about anything.

As I grew into my twenties, I began to realize that their teachings and methods of navigating through life really started to hit home. They also accepted me for who I was even though I took a different life path than theirs. Most important, they never gave up on me. No matter how crazy I got. Through all of these life lessons (and they're still giving me life lessons to this day), having these key people in my life gave me the framework for how I go about my day-to-day life. It also showed me that it is so important to have an excellent home structure and foundation with supportive parents who are a guide and a safety net throughout your life.

I shared this brief story with you to really get you thinking about what your home life looks like. What is your home structure? Do you have family you can go to in times of need or support? Do you trust their opinions and thoughts? Can you brainstorm and dream with them? It is so important to find a mentor in your life. It is also important to have one at home who you can trust. If your home structure isn't set up in these conditions, then please seek outward and look to find somebody who you can connect with on a regular basis who is a positive influence in your life.

It's important to have someone who can guide and mentor you on your professional career, but it's just as important to have a guide on your own personal life journey. I continually thank my mom and dad for all they've done and to help me become the man I am today. I also continuously apologize for my past behavior and actions through that pivotal transformation phase.

Nowadays, we get to laugh about those moments, and we have grown stronger and closer because of them.

Jamar Jones

Thank you, Mom and Dad.

Change Your Circle, Change Your Life

Lesson/Takeaways

What a mentor does is give you guidance and clarity on what you are trying to do. On their own, people's minds only think about what they know or what's in front of them. A mentor opens your mind further. Honestly, I'd say any mentor is going to give you opportunities. You don't need money from people.

You need opportunities to get you to the next level. But you must deliver. You're going to get opportunities that you might not have had before from people who don't even know they're helping you. I'd add Marcus Lemonis to that list. Marcus Lemonis is a serial entrepreneur, TV personality of CNBC's "The Profit" and "Streets of Dreams", speaker and philanthropist. You can Google him and he will come right up for more context. He saw something within me, said execute, and in an hour and a half changed my life. He didn't know he was mentoring me.

No excuses for not having a better circle. If you're trying to go somewhere and you have no mentor. You can google, research, find people you resonate with, and follow them. Understand what they need to bring to the table.

Just try to learn from what they put out. Then take it a step further and see them live. Start digesting and learning from their content. Go into their world.

Doing that will set you up and put you in front of people like them. Your mind will start to think differently. You'll be in different pockets, different circles. You'll find yourself getting closer to where you are trying to go.

Always be the person you're trying to be. Someone is always watching.

Action Items

See who has the influence in the room and figure out how you can provide them with value. Don't ask them to pay you. Don't ask for a favor. Ask for an opportunity. That way, you can improve yourself as well as your chances of having them see your worth and value. They may want to take time to invest in you.

Step 1: Find this person by self-educating. Start by listing people (idols, influencers) who you deem as successful. Learn from them, get their programs, devour their content (programs, seminars, interviews, presentations, videos).

Step 2: Fins three entrepreneurs, celebrities, or other individuals whose messages you love, or who are in an area that you'd like to get into. Digest any type of content they offer, as this will help you pinpoint your future mentor but also it will mold you into finding your path and helping you on your journey.

This will help you in the meantime while you're searching for a direct mentor.

Step 3: Within the next twenty-four hours, identify three individuals who are in the area you're interested in pursuing and whose content you're going to digest for at least five hours a week.

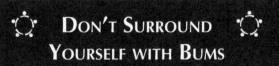

DON'T SURROUND YOURSELF WITH BUMS

We know them and they just keep showing up.

Bums are people who are not motivated. They're negative, complaining, and going nowhere. Or, if they are going somewhere, they don't know where they're going. The type of bum I am speaking of is not a homeless individual. It's someone who aimlessly wanders through life giving nothing back to the world. A bum is someone involved in things that are a negative impact on their life. They're destructive. They never challenge you. These individuals never exercise your mind or provide any form of advice. Bums are the ones who always talk and never listen.

They're many types of bums. You might know the types that live for the weekend. They go out and turn up on Friday, Saturday, and half of Sunday. Maybe they have a job, but every day is miserable for them up to the weekend. They want to do it again every weekend, over and over again. They spend their entire paycheck for the weekend and that's it. I've met so many. They don't challenge you. What are you going to learn in the club? Nothing. The hardest types of bum to get rid of are the bums you genuinely like and enjoy being around. I almost feel bad for them. Almost.

Knowing when to put up barriers

One example of an experience I had with a bum is someone I'd still consider a good friend, but I had to cut ties with him as his mindset wasn't leaving bum-land. I just can't involve myself in that situation. When I started to have that transition in my life, I opened my mind and went deeper, learning about myself and the path I wanted to go. Then I saw him still doing the same thing as always, going out to the club for no purpose, smoking weed and hanging with people who did not promote his growth. They said it was to promote music but really it wasn't. If they got a connection, they wouldn't use it. Putting out music for them was a drag. We only put out music that we did together. They had a negative mindset when I wanted to try something different "It'll never work, you have to be like this, man," Smoking weed daily. Hanging with the wrong crowd. Getting arrested. Not making any changes after that. When I felt I was climbing up the ladder, you're going to start to feel tension. Crabs in a barrel. You're trying to get out and they try to pull you down. They say, "Why are you going so high? We don't know what's out there." You have to break free of this circle. Make a decision: you have to climb out of the barrel, or you will fall back into the bucket. You can't want something more than what they want for themselves. I truly care for him, want more of him, and wanted to continue as friends, but you can't change someone's mindset instantly. Once you have that feeling that you want it more than them, it's time to evaluate. If they are at least listening and soaking in piece by piece of some other paths or opinions, then you have something to work with.

There is another aspect of bums that you need to be aware of. They are easily upset and create drama over nothing. They get angry when you expand your mind by doing what's right for you. That's how you know they're a legitimate bum.

Back to my story. If I wouldn't call this person back within thirty minutes, it was a big deal. If I had things going on that day and missed a call it was like, "Wow, you don't have time for me, man?" As if my world revolves around them. The bums will want you to stay where they're at. There's always some form of tension. You shouldn't have to explain to someone and fight for it every single time. It shouldn't have to be a big thing. In life, you're going to go in all different directions. The real people are going to be the opposite, the ones you don't see for six months and you're still close. They trust you as long as it's not malicious or intentional.

Change Your Circle, Change Your Life

When they constantly need the validation of your relationship, it's not a sincere mutual relationship. They're just spinning in circles and they need that validation from friends, family relationships, and love interests. The funny thing about it is that when they call, it will usually be about nothing. They're takers. I'm not getting anything out of this relationship anymore. We may have common interests, but I feel like they are an anchor holding me in place, and I can't grow as a person around me. You need the right soil, sunlight, and water to grow. And bums are disgusting, damaging insects making a home in the soil, constantly contaminating your growth and foundation.

We haven't talked in a few years and I hear through the grapevine that he is in a similar spot in his life with a few adjustments. I'm not sure much change has happened, but I wish the best for him and I will always be open for a conversation because I do believe in second chances for people.

Bums are in business too. Beware.

On the business side, when I was first starting my business, I was trying anything and everything and I hadn't made a dime. Nothing. I had a website up. I offered fifteen to twenty services. Anything I was good at! That's how you got to start, right? I just knew I needed to move forward.

One of my many offerings was graphic design. So, I'm on Twitter and was sending hundreds of messages daily. Every day. On Facebook, on social media, DM'ing, sending at least a hundred messages per day. And I was selling a graphic with your name or graphic for $5 as I was desperate for a sale. A guy reaches out and says it's cool, he'd like to get one. I said okay, sweet. I tell him it's $5 and he can send it through PayPal. He said, "Okay, I can pay by the end of the week." Then Friday came around and he said he didn't have it yet. "Can you wait a week?" I was like, all right, man, I guess I can wait. In the back of my mind I was thinking, this is 5 bucks we are talking about.

The week went by and he didn't have the payment again. So that was the last time I contacted him.

But when you're dealing with bums, the ones who owe the least amount of money are the biggest headache. They'll be the worst of the worst.

The design I was selling for $5

Change Your Circle, Change Your Life

Lessons/Takeaways

Don't surround yourself with bums because you cannot afford to. Here's why. Every day you spend with these bums it takes away your mental energy, your physical energy, and all of your potential. This is one of the most painful experiences you can go through. Let's say your circle is five core people. Family, friend, relationship. If all five are bums, you'll never succeed. You'll feel negative, run down, unlucky, like things aren't working out. "How come it's not me?" If all five meet the qualifications to be a bum, you won't and can't go anywhere. You will remain in certified bum status.

You can't open your mind. You don't have the time, energy, or resources. The only way is to start limiting time with bums. You have to ween yourself off them. They're like a drug man, and people take them in heavy doses. The real message is you can go cold turkey but that's not recommended. If you cut off five people cold turkey, there could be backlash. Bums are dangerous, especially desperate, angry bums.

If you're in a bad neighborhood you might have real people who act violently to being cut from your circle. Some people are so dangerous, you can't keep taking them in small doses. You really have to limit your time with them. Then find the right time to remove them from your life. See chapter "Find a Mentor." To ask your mentor on advice on how to move forward.

People think, "Oh, I'll deal with it. I can handle the bums." But little do you know, it builds up. Don't motivate the bums as it may lead to retaliation. With family, you can cut them out, though I don't recommend it. If they're just negative, limit interaction. Don't go looking for it. Pull yourself away. When this happens with family, you might learn things about yourself as well and you need to let it go.

Say your dad is negative, but you live there with him. You need to get out of the house and get away. If you are saying you can't because of a financial reason, I would challenge you to say, how many things do you own right now? Are you living beneath your means? Do you really need what you have right now? Because you have to decide on what is most important to you. Every decision has its risks and its rewards.

How long are you going to go down that path thinking they'll change some day? It probably will never happen. So, you have to ween yourself away. You can go on Facebook, find a group of people, read a book about someone who interests you in a positive way. Read it and interact. Get yourself in that space so you can digest some good stuff to start changing your mind. Start washing away all of the junk.

Join my Facebook group and interact with others to Change your Circle, Change your Life.

www.iamjamarjones.com

Change Your Circle, Change Your Life

Action Items

Step 1 - Identify the bums in your circle.

Step 2 - Make a strategy to identify the bums who are in your core/ inner circle and then the acquaintances who are not in your close circle. Use this system.

1. One route is cold turkey; cut them off.

2. Another way is to limit your interaction with the bum. The more you do, the tougher you get and the easier this becomes. Slowly have less contact.

3. Use confrontation. Don't stand for it anymore. You need to confront the bum.

4. Some people in your life you can't cut off because they'll hunt you down. Other times, you can slowly do everything less. Don't show up, don't return calls, confront them respectfully. Tell them you won't be treated like this anymore and you won't take it.

5. Leave them with a choice and an ultimatum. Tell them either change, or they won't be in your life anymore.

Consider this the bum rehabilitation program. The goal is to get all bums out of your inner circle and outer circle. Any new people have to meet your non-negotiables.

Step 3 - After you identify the bums, identify how they got into your life in the first place. Did they change? Did they not change or mature? Are they your family and you were born into the relationship? Did they kind of sneak into your life?

Reading this chapter has hopefully given you the bum repellent you need. However, you will always be challenged. You have to be able to identify bum-like tendencies.

VAMPIRES AND SHEPHERDS

Opening

Before we get into these Vampires and Shepherds, let's talk about energy. Your energy.

Theoretically, everyone wakes up 100%. Then they get hit with whatever comes up. You're late to work so you lose 5% of your energy. You get in and there's a project that is overdue. You get home to screaming kids, you get to spend some quality time with your partner, or you have to call your parents.

All of these things, good or bad, will alter your energy. For me, gratification and milestones both give me energy.

For example, if you just gave 40% of your energy on a presentation you have to do as a speaker but then you get 30% back when you feel jacked! When you're within your purpose, that's how you refill your energy throughout the day. If you're not within your purpose, you're constantly drained. You are not in your purpose if the activity is not fulfilling, is draining, and you're not hitting a milestone or achievement.

There is negative gratification from the wrong things and that can be addictive. You're getting the temporary boost but then it's draining once again. You start at 100% at the beginning of the day but these addictive negative behaviors can actually take you lower than your baseline.

Think about where you're utilizing your energy. If that addiction is the majority of your energy source, you can say, "I'm partying too much. I only get gratification when I'm with my boys at the club. All I want to do is play video games." If you have a big piece of energy that is coming from something that is not growing you as an individual, you can quickly drain your energy without even knowing it.

If you have no "me" time, your battery will drain more quickly as you're not spending any time to yourself.

How much energy should I be putting out? Having awareness is key.

Friends can be one of the biggest drains of Energy!

Let's talk about friends. Man, I have had to change my circle of friends many times. I used to have a best friend that drained so much of my energy. We went to high school together, developed a tight bond, were in the same music group. Had a lot of good times. Good moments. Went through a lot so I definitely felt a tie to him.

Over time, dealing with his unstable, sporadic, chaotic behavior over and over again became very taxing. Even as a friend, you mix that with alcohol and it just became a nightmare. He's already very chaotic as is. A couple times he got drunk and ended up getting lost and we had to go find him. And this happened repeatedly. I had to step into his battles that I had no business being in. I had to be the superman to the relationship. The final straw for me was when he hit on my girlfriend at the time.

It was upstairs, and we were in the same house when he tried to make a move. So, I asked him what the problem was and he kind of waved it off. I went home and he kept talking trash over the next few days. I realized I don't need to be dealing with this. Just because we had a history, I felt like I needed to be there.

After a while, I realized my friendship with him wasn't benefiting me and it wasn't positive. So, I had to cut that tie. That is when I regained and reclaimed my energy. I gave away all that energy for free. I do hope that over the years he has grown from that and is on a positive direction in his life.

Clients can drain you when you least expect it

Not every client is an absolute rock star. A lot of clients will drain energy out of you and your team. They are the ones who will nitpick, request, and pay peanuts. But you wanted the business. If a client is already a pain before they sign, it's likely only going to get worse. I've had situations where clients on video editing did forty revisions on a one-minute video. They paid next to nothing on this video that we went out to film and do post-production (and I know this will make a lot of creatives cringe) and it was all nitpicking with maybe two exceptions that were true revisions.

They also wanted it done ASAP. They will also make their problems, your problems. At the end of the day, you have to be held accountable. You have to give permission for that energy to be used when I signed them as a client. You have to have clients who are a good fit for who you are as a business/company. A lot of times, when you give your energy willingly to certain people, they feel as if you owe them something. So, watch out for entitlement. It can eat you alive.

Vampires. The most dangerous vampires are the ones who are in disguise. They're the closest to you and the ones you love the most, but they're disguised as helpers. They are disguised as a necessity that you need in your life. These are the most dangerous, so be aware. You will spend the majority of your life fighting them. The vampires that are family are the worst ones. When you're just going about your day and you're giving out your energy to your essentials, these vampires come out of nowhere and sneak up on you and take a bite every time. When you least expect it, there is some issue that makes their issue into your issue. You're going about your day and, boom, here they come out of the woodwork.

Vampires don't breathe oxygen; they breathe excuses.

Now your energy has to be used to figure out what this issue is and then go about your day. These vampires are the ones you need to minimize or remove from your life. You will be forever battling "I'm trying to be on the right path, but I keep getting sidetracked," At the end of the day, you are the one responsible for your life and setting barriers, guidelines, and extra garlic!

A lot of people wear turtlenecks to hide the bites from the vampires. They hide the pain because they want to show a composed face and act like everything is under control. But the truth is, they don't. You have to use boundaries and guidelines as garlic. Put up a fortress around your life. You're not letting them in. You're giving them permission to bite you. You're inviting them over to dinner. "Come on in and have a seat. I have a good, cooked meal for you." Every time you invite them in, they see it as an opportunity to say, "I can keep doing this." Until you set boundaries and say, "This is your problem, and you need to take care of it." I understand people don't want others to go down a dark path.

But think about this: Are you and that vampire walking down that dark path together. You need to put up your fortress, get your stakes. You need to be ready for battle. That way, when the vampire shows up, they can't get in. Now they will go on to someone else. Someone who doesn't have the fortress up. When it is a loved one, with maybe a disease, illness, or addiction, their problem is something you need to ask for support if you want to help them. **You need to ask them if they want your help before you try to help them.** Stop trying to put the world on your back and ask for help.

Stop trying to fix all of their issues or sweep them all under the rug. You're not going to be the one to solve everything. You need to get outside help that is reliable and professional. Go to people who you can really rely on. This may take time but go through the proper channels, get it off your shoulders, and get other people involved.

For work, you might not be able to get rid of them. Corporate vampires are the ones where you have the most choice and you have power. You have the power to leave. If you trust in yourself and finish this book, you have the power. Let's say your boss is a corporate vampire sucking the life out of you. You need to set the necessary boundaries, go to HR if it is that serious. Then you need to figure out how much it is worth to you. You have to rank how high of a priority this job is to determine your course of action.

Change Your Circle, Change Your Life

All vampires have a common trait: Complaining. Complaining, complaining, and little to no action. They hate being exposed to the light of truth where they don't even want to face it. They retreat back into the darkness. When the sun comes up, they complain; they don't want to see it. If you have a circle of no vampires and have put up a fortress and a wall, you can fast track your life by so much without these leaches coming after you.

Vampires slow a lot of people down. If you limit your access to these life force-draining creatures, you can more than likely get somewhere five times faster. If you can do that, you're already ahead in the game. If you invite them in, it's over. For example, there are some family issues that happen that I don't get myself involved in. I don't put myself in the situation because now I'm involved in all of the mess.

Drama = Vampire. If you're spending all of your energy on vampires, you're more than likely going to be at a lesser place than someone who is actively managing their energy correctly. You won't even have time to assess your energy because you'll have no energy left. I'm so much happier without the vampires. Going down with them is a slippery slope, When I hear drama, excuses, I no longer really invest myself in it. I'm quiet before I respond. That's even if I do respond.

Shepherds are the opposites of Vampires.

Shepherds. They will take you where you need to go. Shepherds will show you how to navigate your life in the correct way. Whenever I spend time with them, I'm positive, I'm happy, I'm moving forward. They know the path and are the right use of my energy. My conversations with them might turn into great ideas that are very beneficial to my life.

I had a friend I used to work with. I was his manager. After we all got laid off, we spent more time together. He was one who was either cool to hang with and everything was cool, or he would take it to 100 and be difficult—all of a sudden complaining and negative. This started to be the majority of the time. I kept giving him my energy, kept giving him chances.

Eventually, I said enough is enough. I'm not going to continue on this path. I might text back with an "LOL" but that is it. I'm in a point of my life where he's not in the picture. He wasn't a horrible person. He was just negative. Vampires have a certain smell. And it smells kind of bummy.

You can ignore it, you can sweep it under the rug, but eventually it's going to be too much to handle to stay in the room. Whenever it smells like dead dreams in the room, there is a vampire in your midst.

Vampires are drama starters, negative influences, liars, and pathological complainers. The people who need help in a time of need will have something negative going on in their lives, but they may just need support. They are more than likely not vampires. Maybe they just lost their job or their dog, they just went through a divorce. If they are usually positive, this is a time when you can be a Shepherd and help them through a tough time.

Everyone will need help eventually. If people are mainly positive and they're going through a tough time and you have the energy available, you might want to help them out. If people you care about wander into the darkness you might need to pull them out and sprinkle them with holy water! For instance, someone who broke up with their partner a year and a half ago still aren't over it. Might be time to bring them back to reality and have them stop spending their energy on the past.

You have to give them tools and invite them over to the shepherd's side. Some people need a sprinkling of holy water and others need a baptism. Oh, come on, you know the people I'm talking about.

Takeaway/Lessons

To change your circle, you're going to need to evaluate your energy. You will need to know what you're giving your energy to and what's taking from it. Your energy is precious. You need to safeguard it for your own sanity and others. You need to make sure your energy is utilized in the correct places. You have to be aware of where your energy is spent. You need to make sure your circle is filled with shepherds.

You need to make sure your energy isn't being consumed by things that aren't positive and proactive. You need to be aware. These are all about things that you can control. You are choosing to deal with the nonsense. If you're constantly fighting others' battles, how can you fight your own?

Your circle: If you can recognize the amount of energy, you're spending and the amount of energy someone else is spending, you can then navigate what is truly important to change your circle many times, quickly. The thing that slows people down is their direct circle and the inability to manage their energy correctly.

So they constantly have anchors just dragging them along. You want to move your circle fast, because not everybody or every opportunity will be a winner. You have to recognize what is going on quickly, then pivot and make a change.

You get a new job. You think it's a great opportunity. Your manager's manager is a jerk. So your manager is just, "I'm doing whatever this person says." You need to decide immediately, how much energy are you willing to give? Do you have enough to pay bills and move on? Some people pour their energy into things that eventually fizzle out. Think about which the better circle is to be spending your energy and time in. Each circle has a collective energy. If you're hanging out with millionaires, trust me, the energy is different than if you're hanging out with your bum-like friends who want to party every weekend.

Change Your Circle, Change Your Life

Having money doesn't always mean you are spending your energy correctly. One of them could be coked out of their mind and they could still be a vampire. There are still wealthy vampires out there. If you're in a room with C-suite executives, they have worked their way to that position. They might still be powerful vampires.

At PLS was an example of a vampire that came in as a new VP. He sold everyone a dream of how he wanted to do things but had his own agenda in mind. I could smell him and his dead dreams. He ran so many lies to accounting and to so many other people. He embezzled hundreds of thousands of dollars. By this vampire's actions, he actually got forty-five people's lives let go. Let a whole office in Wisconsin be disbanded.

As you can see this destruction can be massive. The key is to navigate it and focus on what you can control.

Control your energy to change your life.

Action Items

Step 1: Write down your energy. Start at 100%, in the morning when you wake up. Your baseline is always at 100%. How much energy do you spend on friends, family, work, extracurricular activities, personal activities? I'm doing this much for work. I'm doing this much for my family. Do this on an average amount on any given day and about a 24-hour time period. Break it down all the way to fill 100%.

Step 2: Look at what you wrote down and see how your energy is aligning with your goals. Base this on your feelings about where your energy is going, not necessarily based on time spent. Are you spending 50% on family? 20% at work? Look at that and say, "What things can I adjust"? Look at your chart and look at your goals.

****To find your goals read "Go for the Championship" and "Life's Not Fair, you have to even out the Odds" ****

Step 3: Determine if your current energy placement is going to help you obtain your goals.

If your energy chart matches up with your goals, great. Keep going. If you see that you are spending too much time in the wrong areas, you need to do some moving around. You need to regularly make note of where your energy is going and adjust accordingly.

Step 4: Time to determine these Vampires and Shepherds. Draw a circle. List the five people who you talk to the most on a regular basis. Write next to their name if you'd consider them a vampire or a shepherd. The idea of this exercise is to identify your vampires and shepherds. Be as hard on yourself as you can. You know who is draining your energy and who is adding energy. If 50% or more of your circle are vampires, you are in trouble and you need to figure out ways to get rid of them.

Change Your Circle, Change Your Life

See "Don't Surround Yourself with Bums."

You're going to always have encounters with vampires and bums but don't invite them in. Get your stakes. Get your garlic. If half of your circle are vampires, you need to look in the mirror at yourself. If you can't see your reflection, ask yourself, "Am I a vampire?" Your goal is to have your entire circle be shepherds.

See "Find A Mentor" and "Winging It."

You need to replace these vampires with shepherds.

Step 5: Draw a battery. On the left side, write down a list of a few things that drain your battery. It could be a person, an activity, any other negative force. On the right side, write down the things that provide you with energy.

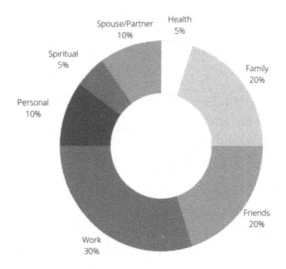

☼ YOU LLC ☼

You LLC because YOU are a business. It's time for YOU to build your brand.

I think personal brand is everything for individuals to stand out and differentiate themselves in the market and all aspects of their lives. A **personal brand** is a widely recognized and largely uniform perception or impression of an **individual** based on their experience, expertise, competencies, actions and/or achievements within a community, industry, or the marketplace at large. **Personal** brands may be deliberately modified to reinvent a public persona.

You need to announce your brand. Get on the horns. Shout it from the rooftops and use a megaphone. Let people know your brand. If you're not building it yourself, how are people going to connect you to things? How will they think of you when something pops up? People lose themselves in their occupation, and not in a good way. Their brand is just, "the guy who works here." "The woman who works there." But who is that? You're not setting yourself apart. You're not branding yourself outwardly, personally.

You need to do that because then people will start to associate you with other things. Personal branding honestly needs to be taught in school.

Especially business. Even in an interview, you carry your brand with you. A lot of things can be branded. If you came into an interview, depending on the position...I'm talking about a full suit. I'm already getting a certain image and brand of who you are.

Like my good friend now Carlos who worked with me on the same team at my IT job. He loves to come in fully decked out. That is like his brand. He was known as the dude who was fresh. That stands out to me when hiring someone. Even though it's not everything. You could've worn slacks, polos, or jeans. He came in suited and booted. But that branding is so important for an individual to announce who they are and what makes them different.

What does a business do? Build brand. We as people need to build brands and we're building them whether we want to or not. Regardless of what you think. People are analyzing and putting you into categories. Putting you into lanes. They're already evaluating you. You have to ask yourself...

Do you want to control your brand? Or do you want others to control it for you?

How YOU are unique and unlike anyone else

Business-wise, branding is everything. Branding is the long game. It's what you want at the end of the day, for people to know you for a certain thing. When we start working with someone at Foureva Media, we walk them through and discover what makes them different. What sets them apart and makes them unique? What's their value add?

We get clear on their identity and also their visual presentation. Shouting it from the rooftops, who you are and what is your brand. We'll take someone who is unclear on that concept and show them how to get it out there. People will start to recognize you and come to you for that. The brand is everything. The more you push it out there, the more people will come to you. Just like people recognize top brands. Nike, Amazon, Gucci. They hit the pavement to let people know who they are and what they stand for. If they take their foot off the gas a little, it'll still go. Like for yachts. They don't do huge commercials for super yachts. They don't do commercials for Ferrari. There's no Black Friday sale for yachts.

After you build your brand and are recognized for something, then people can recommend you. For instance, when a service you provide can satisfy a need someone else has.

Here's the goal, people: You want to be in people's heads. Like the telepath from the comics named Professor X. That's where the magic happens. We like to get that done up front so that you are known for something. If I rattled off your favorite brands, your favorite sports players, your favorite singers, your favorite speakers, they've branded themselves a certain way where they have connected you to their brands.

Here is the difference between someone who built a brand and someone who is just selling. Let's say two people are trying to find a job. The person with no brand is just knocking on doors and asking, are you hiring? Are you hiring? They do their pitch and then wait. But they have no identity to go with them.

The other person who has built a brand doesn't necessarily have to knock on doors. People come to them and help connect the dots for them. So, who do you think it's easier to get a job or employment from? The more you're recognized, the more value you have.

These two people are not equal. One has a brand. One doesn't. Even in your personal life, you have to build your brand. Are you the person always sad and depressed, or are you outgoing? Are you too critical? How are you branding yourself? Don't you want to be in control of your own brand? This is not something you can say "isn't for me." The key is, the more people who know about you and your brand, the greater chance you have. So you have to get it out there, shout it out, make it known. The more people who know about your brand, the more opportunity you have.

Use your Uniqueness to your Advantage

I believe my brand is video; people will associate me with video. I have defined myself also as always wearing my hat no matter the occasion or setting. I remember when Marcus Lemonis (See Chapter

Change Your Circle, Change Your Life

"Find a Mentor" for description on who this is" said something about my hat when I was in the room with him during the business session. He said something about the Foureva Productions hat I was wearing. It was on the live stream. Something about "lose the P, it's all F" or something like that. I laughed but wasn't too thrilled.

The hat sometimes stands out so much. It could be a goatee or a big beard. You can brand yourself in different ways. I always just leaned into having the hat. Another part of my brand is motivation. Even back when I did music and bridging people together, I did motivational music. Something that will get some juice and fire in you and have you go and get it. I get associated with marketing and social media. People probably see me as a face of social media marketing. Just because that's where people see me. I'm always on those platforms. They put 2 and 2 together.

As an individual, you have a career you want to pursue. A company can give you the tools, resources, connections, and networks to help you build your personal brand. But don't let that company just completely absorb your own company and brand. You LLC. **An LLC is a way you can register your business. Limited Liability Company. It's a way to let the government know you are a legit business.**

That also has to be in your top priority. So, let's say your path is that you wanted to be a sales manager for a car dealership. Instead of being just for that dealership, why not be the go-to person for cars. Know the how-to's, what to recommend, what to do, and what not do.

The more people who know of you, the more likely they'll bring you more opportunities. Being a sales manager, you can outwardly promote your personal brand. The more you build your personal brand, the more beneficial you can be to the company. No matter what, you have to be known for something. Even if you have your own business, you're in the business of you.

Jamar Jones

Lessons/Takeaway

When you're not around, what people think of you is your brand. If you want to change your brand, you have to start asking yourself some real hard questions about what you represent. Who is your target audience? What are your core values and beliefs? What do you want to be known for five years from now? What do people say about you when they have to explain you to someone else? Who are the target people who engage in your brand? What are their age and occupations? Who are the people who are interested in your brand? What are their interests and goals?

Another thing is, if you had to put your brand into images, what would it look like? Everyone has heard of a vision board. In marketing we do a mood board. Mood boards take what you want your brand to represent visually. Images, fonts, colors, graphics, quotes, everything to describe your brand awareness today and what you want it to be. You do it in an imagery fashion. So, it's not just words. It's something I can see. This is my current brand. Where do I want to go? What do I want to be known for? Lastly, what are the key benefits that someone can get from my brand?

Then you dive into the why? Why you? Why are you doing what you're doing? Do people trust your brand enough that they'd recommend it to others? What are the strengths of your brand and what are the weaknesses? "Well, I wouldn't go to them for this. But I'd definitely go to them for this." In business, it's frowned upon to curse up a storm. But serial entrepreneur and social media guru, Gary Vaynerchuk doesn't care, and he can curse up a storm. He built up a brand and it has hurt and helped him at the same time. If you push through, enough people will get on board. Enough people have broken the cliché that you have to be the older, white dude in a three-piece suit. Now people know that success looks different today. The same is true with tattoos. No longer is it, "You're not getting hired because of that tattoo" because more people have broken through this barrier.

Humans have branded themselves since the beginning of time. Signs, photos, language. They're trying to represent and be something. Everyone wants to be or attract that attention. Even the people who want to shy away, that's a certain type of brand. They're loners. They sit by themselves at the lunch table. You have to ask yourself, "What is my brand going to represent?" High school is the biggest brand expression that you can get. It's so clear. I could go into any high school and know the brands. The way they talk, the way they dress, the activities they are in, how they handle themselves. Especially when I was in high school, nothing changed except the people, and maybe the environment and area you're in. Maybe different groups but everyone is just branding themselves. And no school program teaches this. It's just human nature. That is what is crazy. We want to brand ourselves.

Do you want to be in charge of your own brand? You're being

associated with your brand no matter what. Just being you is the key. If you want to be you and unique and not the status quo, you don't want to act like everyone else in your circle.

No other person on this earth is you. You have unique characteristics and qualities that no one else has. The more you lean into that, the more people will try to copy. People mimic. The key is, don't copy. Just be yourself. Find yourself and you'll find what is unique.

Ask a few coworkers, a few friends, a few family members. Jot down how they'd describe you to someone and sum you up for someone who has never met you. Find the similarities in their descriptions as they may vary by circles. Through that, you can probably see the different ways people view you. The brand will change, and your day ones might view you differently. You further your brand the more you interact. Branding takes time. The word originates from literal animal branding. What is seared into your skin that you are known for? That is branding. Branding is not just one experience. If someone has only had one interaction with you, they could make assumptions about your brand by that one interaction.

Your brand will determine which circles you're allowed into and which circles you are not. It's important that your brand have consistency, that the people in your circles are screaming and shouting out the same message. Consistency.

If your brand starts to build a bad reputation, you will actually close a lot of doors and opportunities for yourself. Let me tell you, most times bad reputations spread a lot faster than good ones. When you're looking at your circle, look at your brand but also the brands with which you're associated. Your brand might be swallowed up by other people's brands because of all of the negatives.

For example, you got straight A's, you're in a ton of school activities, you're a positive individual, you're always happy. But your direct circle who you hang out with after school are a bunch of drug addicts.

Change Your Circle, Change Your Life

That's their brand. They skip school, smoke a ton of weed. If you're known to hang out with them all the time, you could be deemed one of them. Even if that is not your true self. You need to make sure you're in the right circles and in the right place. If you're trying to control the narratives for your life, you need to be very serious and intentional about who you're around.

If only good things come from you and good things are said about you, it will continue on and on and on. If you're in a bad circle, you're going to be associated with other bad circles as well. Because now people know you and you can't be trusted.

Look how this cycle can start of branding yourself. Let's say you start getting into weed and now at parties someone asks you if you want to take some pills. You start taking them and become addicted without even realizing it. Now all of a sudden, this is affecting your life and you start under performing at your job. Then let's say you lose your job. Then your trust is starting to slip with your loved ones. Then you lose your spouse. All this time your developing a brand that you can't be trusted and the drugs are in control. Then you're homeless somewhere. Now your reputation is, "I don't know where they are; they can't be trusted." To get out of that, you need to make huge, life-altering decisions to rebrand yourself.

There is no way instantly to flip the script and change what people think of you. It's possible but you have to make some drastic decisions.

Jamar Jones

Action Items

Step 1 - Write down and identify what you think your personal brand is. What are you known for? What do people know you as? Then ask a family member, ask a coworker, ask your partner, ask an acquaintance, and ask a mentor, "If you had to describe me as a brand to someone else, what would you say?"

Ask the question and shut up. You're here for perspective. You're here to take notes. Don't ask them any leading questions. Write down the answers from each of the people you ask and soak them in.

Step 2 - Ask them, "If you had to describe me to your employer, how would you describe me?" You have to prep this person and tell them that they can be honest, open, and truthful to you. "What are five areas where I fall short? Be honest; you won't offend me." Then shut up. Ask these questions to the same people as in step 1 but also to a variety of people from different backgrounds and age groups. This is your discovery phase of what your current brand is.

Step 3 - Think about your future brand and what you want to be known for. Look at what things need to change in order to obtain this new brand image and how you can change your messaging. How can you change your positioning to promote your new message? What do you have to do in order to change the perception of your future brand?

Write those things down and now live it. Be consistent. Once you change your brand, everything you do has to have a consistent message. See this chapter for a future check-in to see where your current brand is at.

Step 4 - Ask people again and see where they think your brand is now. You're looking for the common denominators. If three out of five people mention something about you, it might be true. Whether it is true or not, this is your brand. This is what you're putting out into the world. Take your feedback with a grain of salt. If you receive feedback that you don't want to hear, this can often come from denial. Make sure that you're open minded and humble enough to take the feedback.

BACK DOOR

I'd rather take the back door and get escorted in.

You have to go through the back door if you want to be successful.
Going to the front door is for chumps. Do you want to be treated
as general public or a VIP specialty case? The back door gives you
unlimited access to the people who you need to reach and who give
you that credibility and necessary clout. If you can't directly get in
the back door, you target the person you're trying to reach, and you
get inside their network. This is crucial because it validates you as a
business, as a person who is serious. You're one who can be worked
with.

My backdoor method has worked in many aspects of my life and I have
found it transfers from business to professional entrepreneurship,
even to getting the woman of your dreams. Hey, if you want to talk
to her, get to know her friends, and eventually she has no choice but
to talk to you.

Persistence and Approach will earn you access to the Back Door

I had a situation where I was trying to get into the Wisconsin National
Speakers Association chapter. A lady by the name of Julie was the
president of this chapter at the time and I was trying to pitch an idea
to her that could be very beneficial to their chapter. I knew it could
be an entry point for us to work with a lot of new potential clients
as well.

I was following up with Julie for several months with little to no
interaction (a few emails here and there) and one phone call. Julie
was just so busy and, honestly, I don't think my request, my ideas,
and my pitch were a top priority for her.

So I had a choice to make. She wasn't calling or emailing me back.

Change Your Circle, Change Your Life

Either I give up or figure out how else to approach it. Either I directly send an email, or I call the NSA directly. That approach would have been going through the front door. I'd more than likely get a generic response and be placed to wait in line with everyone else. I needed to think of another way to get this done.

Then something interesting happened. I went through the back door.

I had a client named Jeff Kortes who talked about the NSA all the time. Maybe I could have a conversation with him and see how to get involved. That way I can figure out who I needed to talk to directly.

He introduced me to one of his connections. His name was Phil Gerbyshak, a well-renowned speaker, sales trainer, and LinkedIn guru. Phil Gerbyshak got me in touch with several other speakers in the organization who ended up becoming clients of ours. These clients were already in the same circle as Julie. This component is very important because it validates you; now you're involved in her circle.

Phil did a presentation with the NSA and talked up my company. He said we were going to film him. "By the way, my next gig is coming up and I'll be in person. I will have a video crew, Foureva Productions, filming me." Talking us up to the organization made a huge impact. I told him that we're trying to get into the NSA. I didn't directly ask him to get us into the NSA. Phil had us do a gig. I was unpaid, but it got me in the door.

As soon as we walked into the event, we were surrounded by multiple people. They said, "We know so much about you guys. We've heard about you and heard you're a go-to company for videography. Do you want anything, bagels, coffee?" Phil's credibility in the circle gave us credibility which automatically turned the key to people accepting us before they even saw any "proof."

After the event, everyone talked about us and the word spread.

We had another client who was going to eventually become the president of this organization.

At this point, so many people were aware of our company in the circle that Julie could not ignore us anymore.

We had credibility by the time we even got to the event.

We still get clients from those connections till this day.

From Crowds of a few to Thousands

One example of me using the backdoor method is when I was still pursuing my music career. I was becoming super frustrated trying to book shows. I was doing stuff here and there, little, rinky-dink, smaller performances. For some performances, I actually had to pay to perform.

I was getting pretty tired of finding places to perform. I was always sending emails or calls to the club or bar owners or promoters. I had been doing it for years and I was starting to wonder if I wanted to keep doing this for years. Then when you finally book something, you have to promote the event and get people there.

It dawned on me; how do I get through the backdoor? Who do I know who needs entertainment? Where are a lot of people? Who would be interested in my message?

Then I thought: Colleges. They have a lot of people who would be willing to listen to new music. Okay, how do I get in there? I can't just walk in and do a show. So, then I said, what can I attach myself to? I started brainstorming ways to get attached to things colleges would do.

My research pointed me to cancer awareness. I tell this to upcoming artists all the time. Don't just make it about music. Attach yourself to other causes as well that are bigger than you. I attached myself to cancer research and survival. I already knew people who suffered from the effects of cancer; some even passed away from it. So it was a close-to-home topic for me. I wanted to support with my share.

I found that there are student groups in colleges that have budgets that they have to use, or they will go away. I started making a crazy number of calls and emails, sending at least fifty to a hundred emails a day and at least fifteen to forty calls a day to colleges all over Wisconsin and the East Coast.

The cool thing is that I got responses back quickly from people who referred ne to someone else who ran that aspect of the planning. I asked if I could perform at the Relay for Life events. The cool part is these events are all across the country. When the first one said yes, I was just blown away. My first Relay for Life event was absolutely bonkers. It was in Superior, Wisconsin of all places! Small town on the tip of Wisconsin, six-hour drive for me from Milwaukee. I booked that and they paid for my hotel, paid for me to perform and, not only that, since I had booked a gig with the school, I started to book other gigs around the college as well. Now this is where the snowball effect happens.

I booked and performed at the largest nightclub in Wisconsin. I just told them that I was trying to find somewhere to bring all of these people to after the show. You can't just walk in and say, "Yeah, man,

I have dope music. Your audience will really like it." They don't care about that.

They want to know if you can bring people in and do you add value to what they already have?

Do you have leverage? Leverage wins. Begging loses.

So not only did I get paid, and a paid hotel stay, I also performed at two places in one night. Almost everyone from the college event came to the club afterward. In total, about sixty people from the Relay for Life event came to the nightclub. I was the only performer there that night other than the DJ.

To end this story and press the fast-forward button. I did over two hundred shows after this. I started with maybe thirty shows a year if I was lucky. Maybe twenty shows at some rinky-dink, smaller places or paying for spots that weren't cheap.

I went from that to doing over a hundred shows per year, performing at all different colleges in the Midwest and the east coast.

Stop banging your head trying the front door method.

The back door works.

Change Your Circle, Change Your Life
Connections and Relationships are key cards to the Back Door

The reason I got the PLS opportunity, and I was able to get hired is because of the backdoor approach. If I had submitted my application, gone through Monster.com, and waited for people to call me, I would've never been chosen.

I didn't have qualifications, the schooling, anything on paper for IT support work. And I was only nineteen-years old.

But I had a friend whose mom worked at this company. She saw my potential and knew I had messed with computers in the past. She said, hey, might as well give him a shot, and vouched for me. She co-signed me to get that job for Rick by saying, "Why not bring him in?" I didn't have an interview, my hat was cocked, I was wearing baggy jeans, and I came with a friend.

I walked around and met Randy Wilinski (Randy now works with me here at Foureva Media). Randy was answering five phones at the same time when I first saw him. Not even kidding! He was dedicated!

I got a fifteen-minute talk with the boss and that got me some face time as well. I called a week later after the interview to ask if I had the job and they said yes. I don't think it was because of me. It was really because of my friend's mom. She vouched for me and said give him a shot. I would've loved to have been in that room to hear what she said about me.

Later in life I learned that he also gave me a shot because Randy didn't have any experience in IT at the time either and he was impressing the manager so much that he was comfortable to do this again.

You have to go through the back door to be successful. The front door is for chumps. The back door gives you unlimited access to people you need to reach and also provides the necessary clout and credibility.

Jamar Jones

Lessons/Takeaways

Look at where everyone else is going and find an alternative route. If everyone is doing this, you need to think, "How can I get around this barrier and still make it happen?" If everyone is submitting an application, how else do you get in?

I knock once and then I go for the back door all day. It's important to mention what I call The Mafia Reference.

When everyone is trying to get customers, they do the blanket approach. The easy, front door approach. This approach is what businesses normally do. The best way to get into the building is the back door/mafia way—but I don't mean by killing, gambling, violence, manipulating, or blackmailing. I'm talking about the stereotypical gangster movie relationships and how they are built.

They shake hands, build rapport, do favors in exchange for other favors. They're all about 1:1 interaction and personal relationships. Build that rapport and get as much face-to-face time as you can. Be strategic about it but go face to face with the big initiatives that you're trying to achieve.

Think of the relationships that the mafia builds and the bonds that they make. You have to go in like the mafia. That is the way I've built my business. If you do good things in the world, good will come back to you. Build relationships with people who can get you on the inside.

Change Your Circle, Change Your Life

Action Items

Step 1- Approach a current problem by first acknowledge what and where the front door is. See what everyone else is doing and find a way to differentiate yourself. Everyone is submitting/applying here, speaking to the manager. What else are they doing? Acknowledge what everyone else is doing.

Step 2 - Research other people who are involved in the area that you're trying to get into and who already have access to the "building." After that, find a way in. You have to connect with them and add value to what they're doing or at least know how to get involved.

I got connected to a guy who has worked at CBS 58 for the past seven years. I connected with him years ago. This is an example of finding someone who can walk you through the front door. I was already in the same field as him and he wanted to connect, to chop it up, share ideas, talk about production. We saw each other's recent work and knew we could add value to each other. I wasn't targeting that specific TV station, but I was targeting production professionals in general. I wanted to connect with them because, if they needed help with any work, I could be a resource. I messaged him back and forth to build a relationship. We connected on LinkedIn, engaged on social media.

Step 3 - Build a personal connection. Make a phone call, attend a meeting, join a networking group. Start showing up. That's how you get into the circle. Research. See what they like. So, my connection from the new station reached out and said they were starting a new series and asked if I wanted to come into the station to talk. I literally went through the back door when I got there. He opened the back door of the building for us to walk through together. It was a dark alley with lowlights. This is very important, and it is the next step for the backdoor method: having someone walk you through the back door. Through our conversations, they will get you access to the buildings. You might have to ask if they don't. After you build rapport, the ask comes naturally. "Hey, can you maybe ask the station to be a go-to film production company that you can work with?" Never be afraid to ask but make sure you're providing value to them as well.

**To really make this effective, you really have to address and read – "Winging It," "Urkel meets Stefan", "You LLC," and "You ain't Working Hard."

You have to have the right soft skills. If you're not providing value, it might be uncomfortable to ask. Try to make sure you're mutually beneficial. Build a connection and try to understand what their needs are. You can't just say, "I want to meet Beyonce." Everyone wants to meet Beyonce, so why would they help you do it? You have to have a skillset, money, a connection. This is a rinse and repeat process for each goal. It's not sucking up; it's more finessing and adding value. Sometimes you will absolutely have to suck up or suck it up.

You may have to work with people who you might not have chosen to work with; but to get to your goals, you have to humble yourself, smile, nod, and kiss babies. You need to make these connections to move on to your next journey. They are a roadblock in a way, and you'll need to get over them in order to proceed to the next step. Treat everyone as if they could be your next opportunity.

At times you're going to have to play politics and be a politician in a way. You won't want to necessarily hang out with and be in the same circle as all of the keyholders to the "building" but, in order to get in the back door, you might have to do a bit of finessing and people pleasing.

Everything you could ever want is waiting for you. All you have to do is open the back door.

YOU AIN'T WORKING HARD

Work Ethic is the Ultimate Competitive Advantage in Life.

Been using this saying for years: You ain't working hard. When I first started my business. I put this tagline on T-Shirts because I loved the concept so much.

I created it because my view point is most people's work ethic was soft. Analyzed how they were operating. I was like, okay, well...my tagline will be, "You're not doing enough".

It really stemmed from Grant Cardone. 10x your mindset. **He has grown a whole movement from 10X and you really should look into if you haven't heard this before. Highly recommend it.**

When I was reaching out to four hundred people in a week, I didn't have an option to not work hard. It was motivation for me to keep going. I had just started the business and I had no nights off. I kind of put it out there in the world to let myself know I needed to be doing that. I had to build the business. It was just me. I was laid off from my corporate gig and I had to make it happen. I put it out as a tagline not just for myself but for everyone else.

I'm not saying burn yourself out and I wouldn't prescribe the pill I took. I was working until 4 a.m. and just going. You have to think about your effort level. Whatever level you want to achieve, you need to work harder than that. You have to become obsessed.

If you think 2x is enough, you now need to do triple that to be successful.

Let me ask you, "When has just doing enough ever been enough?" Never.

You have to keep building, building, shoot, shoot, shoot to score. You need to raise the bar. But, you may say "Jamar, I'm always working, and I don't have any more time to give!" If you're always working? Work harder. Feelings will get you in trouble. If you feel as if you're doing everything you can, you're not doing enough or you're not doing it the right way.

There have definitely been times when I've gone 100mph in the wrong direction. This philosophy is more about the effort level and what you're trying to get. The reason I was able to book a hundred shows a year was because of the effort level I was putting in, pointed in the right direction.

Back when I was working at PLS, I'd take calls over the lunch break to book shows for my music. How many calls can I get in an hour? I'm going to get through at least thirty right now. I knew I wanted a certain result. If you think you're only going to be able to hit ten calls a month and you have to hit your sales number but you're only putting out a couple hours a month, you're not going to get it.

The truth is 80% of people aren't working hard enough. You need to triple or 4x your output if you feel as if you're working hard enough and not seeing the results you'd like. It's not about the hours. It's not you have to stay up until 4 a,m. Whatever you think you need to be doing, you need to multiply that. The symptoms of working hard are, seeing results and seeing opportunities.

Here is the key and I think everyone needs to know this. If you're trying to get somewhere, you're not going to typically see results until after three months. You have to put in the effort for at least three months. Don't say "I'll kill it for this week" and expect results to come. You have to put in at least three months minimum to start seeing some results.

4 Four Hundred

(My stage name was 4-0 *pronounced four oh* and would make 400 new connections a week)

Change Your Circle, Change Your Life

When I started my business, the struggles were that the bank account wouldn't last forever even though I had some money saved. Since I had just gotten laid off my previous job, I had some reserves saved up to carry me a few months. I had to get people to know about me and what services I offered. I had twenty-five to thirty services when I started. I had to figure out what would work and then do it again and again.

First, I started on the entertainment side making beats and instrumentals for artists. What happened was I could only sustain that so much. Even though I was reaching out to so many people (hundreds of emails per day). After three months, I had gotten one or two people to bite. I did artist consultations, and I had more demand on the video and photo side coming in. I took those three months and then pivoted into photos and videos. I had sent so many messages, probably already thousands, until I met DJ Payday via Twitter. DJ Payday is a known sound engineer and DJ in the city of Milwaukee. If you really think about it, it took me months of hard work to get up to DJ Payday.

DJ Payday was one of the sole reasons I went from just starting to meeting more people. DJ Payday: I want to shout him out in my book.

Jamar Jones

He's such a good guy. He introduced me to P Rock aka Promise who is a good friend of mine now and worked at a local radio station; Sky McCloud, a fashion stylist and artist 40Mil, a beat maker and producer; Jack Harlow, who is now a giant Grammy nominated major artist in hip hop, Sean Smart, a graphic designer and artist; B Justice, one of the top artists from Milwaukee; and so many others.

A ton of people in the city who were there, and he was the opportunity that spawned from all of this. Other opportunities were clicking but he saw I had done a lot already and he opened up a whole new circle of people I needed to meet. He was my back door as he had already put himself in it.

That got me in the back door as he was already seen as a person who was valued in that community. He gave me access to those people.

He is really the sole reason that I know people in the city. He doesn't want any shine (credit), or accolades. He just wants to watch the magic happen and see people succeed. We passed off intros to each other. If I knew of someone who needed beats, I'd pass their name over to him. He actually kickstarted the video side of my business in the beginning. Filming at the radio station for P-Rock aka Promise. He is a radio personality that was looking for content to promote the work he was doing in the city of Milwaukee.

Then I filmed my first music video was for a local artist in Milwaukee for $500.

I didn't know what I was doing. That was the first official video I did. It was a big moment for me.

To get these results I needed to do more, more, and more.

To get anywhere in life, I feel like a lot of people's effort level and expectations don't match up. They say "I need to find a job"...okay, cool. Tell me what your process is for finding a job. They say "Well, I put some stuff on Monster, Indeed, and Facebook but I want this dream job." And that's all they're doing. They took level one action

115

and expected level ten results. Then what happened? Three months go by and they say "No one is calling me back. I had one interview and it didn't go anywhere. I don't know what is going on.".

Those are the results you'll get, if that's the effort you put in. Crickets. My process would be, first, to do the basics. Then I would post constantly that I'm looking for a job. Talk to at least a hundred people a day. ask them who they know. Everyone has family and a circle of friends. I would go to schools, just trying to connect with people in the area of industry I was interested in. Go to network meetings about that field. Hit the pavement. You have to show everyone that you are looking for a job. Shout it from the rooftops. You'll be surprised at the results you can achieve.

School was not my strong suit but looking back I could of done more.

Academically, I sucked. School was miserable for me. The system forces you to learn a certain way. It didn't cater to my strengths. I'm horrible at math. My brain doesn't work the same way as other people's brains.

I should have acknowledged that and worked way harder. I went to summer school every summer. Four times. All for math. I was behind all the time in math. If I wanted to earn a C or a B or a passing grade, I had to do a maximum effort to get the output and results I wanted for that passing grade. If I did the bare minimum for me, I would have failed.

I was forced to do more. At least if I wanted to not be held back a grade. I passed because I put in the time (probably more than other kids).

But looking back, I needed to alter my efforts and not wait until the universe made me do it.

Do you want to wait for the heart attack or eat healthy now? Do you want to wait to be homeless later or do the work to get a job now?

Lessons/Takeaways

If you want something and want a certain result for it, you need to put in the effort for it and then times that effort by four. Shoutout Grant Cardone, Mr. 10X. Multiply it way more than what is reasonable.

When *people who challenge your work ethic (they say you're working too much or too hard) are oftentimes looking at themselves in the mirror and are upset about what they haven't achieved.*

Performance + No Results = Not Working Hard Enough!

(Either Not hard enough or not smart enough) See Chapter "Back Door" for more ideas on your approach.

Change Your Circle, Change Your Life

Action Items

Step 1: Write down the top five goals you're already working. They can be the same five goals as from another chapter or you can write down your top five goals now.

Step 2: Write down all the things you're currently doing to meet this goal. Spend ten minutes writing them all down.

Step 3: Take the effort you're currently exerting and multiply it by four. You probably need more but this is to figure out how much action you need to take to try to achieve your goals. You've done ten interviews this month? You need to be doing forty. Look at how many actions you do per week. Then break it into per day.

You have to be actively trying to achieve these goals.

You need to be educated enough in these areas to be applying it to your goals.

If you're continuously not achieving the results you seek after applying these results, you may need to read chapters, "Find a Mentor," and "Urkel meets Stefan" and "Back Door."

This is pure effort and mindset. You need to keep increasing your effort or you need to be working smarter.

Going for the Championship

Go for the Ring, not Gameday Stats.

It's the idea of playing the long game and not being satisfied with short-term victories. Short-term victories are great but what is your ultimate goal? You have to craft your plan for the long haul, not just quick fixes. Example: You lock in a new client as a business owner. The short game would be to go on vacation, treat yourself to something, soak in your success without thinking about "How do I scale and duplicate this again and again and save it for safekeeping?"

The analogy is Basketball. If you have one person who is all about themselves, wants points, ball hog, they're not going for a championship: they're going for a highlight reel. They're not trying to grind their way to the top with a team.

Sacrifice is a part of the seeing bigger picture.

When you start a business, you need to be in it to win the championship. You can't start by proclaiming, "Oh, I want more time and freedom. I want a fancy car. I want champagne dreams." If you do, you're setting yourself up for failure. When I started my business, my goal was to create something bigger than myself. I wanted to get a certain level of power to be able to help more people. When you're at a certain status and you've built something from the ground, a machine that can run you can empower others. At the end of the day, I want to leave a legacy and leave my stamp on the world. That's how I started.

Then you get into the reality of, "I just got to pay bills." Going through that, there were some pitfalls and some wins. Within the first five years, I had wins but I confronted pitfalls as well. Some of my wins didn't come in the form of money; they came in experience. People need to understand that education is expensive.

I had over twenty services and didn't know which ones would take off. I actually started two companies: Innovision, an IT consulting company that lasted about two months; and Foureva Productions, a video production company. I had started the two businesses simultaneously. Innovision was a company I opened with old coworkers. They put in work for about two weeks and then they dropped like flies. When everyone dropped out, I asked myself, "Do I really want to do this?" At the same time, I was messing around with starting Foureva Productions. I would sell some beats on the side, but it wasn't formal at this point. I was just trying to figure out what I wanted to do. There were many moments when I could've quit.

After my initial cash ran out after about seven months, that's when the photography and videography took off. I was doing artist consulting and some beat production. But the video services were what people wanted the most. I kept building a bigger network so people would come to me for videography services. About two years into my business, I had a crucial decision to make. This is why I say, you have to be in it for the long haul. You might get lucky and have a couple of successes, but I had just started to switch to more of a corporate focus rather than doing a lot of work for entertainment space.

All of a sudden like at the end of fall in November 2017, all the jobs stopped. No one contacted me for some reason. It was like someone pulled the plug and everything dried up. I was in the worst position financially, business wise. My heat was cut off for a long time. I got myself into a lot of debt. At that moment I seriously considered getting a job. I said things like "This might not be for me, " or "Do I keep pursuing this and pivot and find a different way?" Because I can't have this happen again. Thankfully my parents helped me out because I was in over my head. It took a lot for me to ask. I am not one to ask for assistance with money. It's not in my DNA.

This was from end of fall to beginning of spring. Total of four months of nothing. I'm sharing this just to show the type of stamina you have to have when running a business.

Be in it for the long haul. I changed a lot of processes to make sure the next winter this wouldn't happen to this degree. I changed up again, got focused. and then for the next two years I perfected my game plan and model. I kept getting better. It's just like the time you spend shooting in the gym. I have to get my reps in. Who am I targeting? What is my client base? How is my website? What else can I do to get my marketing and my business processes right?

From then on, I got deeper into the business world. As a result, I got more and more out of it. So how do I reach more people and cast a net instead of fishing with a spear? And that's when it switched for me. I already did this for music and now I just did it for my business. I started to work with conferences, trade shows, events. Then I thought, "How do I attract more speakers.'. I created this process that got us into a lot of conferences and in front of a lot of speakers. We were able to monetize that, and it actually got my business through the next two years.

After about four years of business, we kept running into the issue of doing amazing videos for our clients but seeing them not using them "correctly" or not utilizing them to their full potential. We wanted to tell clients, "Hey, we can really help you use these with brand recognition, marketing, and tactics." That's when we started Relatable Marketing. We created that business to have more skin in the game and to show there were other ways to help companies other than just videography.

I had a business partner at the time; both of us pushed the business. Fast forward a year into that, and we had been through so many ups and downs especially during unforeseen times. One day in August,

Change Your Circle, Change Your Life

I was feeling frustrated overall with business and the effort going into it on my side. I was watching Marcus Lemonis, CNBC host of the TV show *The Profit*, live on Instagram, where he gives advice to small businesses. I've been following Marcus for a while; he is one of my top five experts who I look up to. I agree with his philosophy and look to him for guidance and advice.

Also, I saw him speak a couple times (once in Chicago at a trade show, where we took a picture together; and another in Chicago at the Ascend event while he was doing a keynote). I've always tried to get onto his radar or into his circle. I had seen his live feeds before on his Instagram but that day I wanted to just crash for the night. I was playing video games to unwind and was going to do exactly that. But something got into me. I took my phone, went into the office, and watched the last twenty minutes of the live stream.

He was going to pick one more person on his livestream and I was the last one who he selected! I went on his livestream, talked to him, and he said he wanted to bring us in to chat about our business and how he could help. Fast forward two days later and we got a two-hour business coaching session from Marcus Lemonis! Exciting, right?!

Well, he absolutely respectfully tore us apart on that livestream. It's all available to watch and everyone can see us get chewed out.

He dove into core aspects of our partnership, what our business principals were as a company and how to explain what we do to others.

It was such a game changer for me. Not only did we get chewed out... he gave us a business opportunity to prove ourselves! Absolutely an amazing experience that I will forever be grateful for.

During that experience, I felt as if this was a playoff game win. I had gone through so much during my five years of business that I needed that win. Just for the validation, the experience, the expertise he gave off. Marcus said, every business needs a shot and a break. Just that one chance to get over that hump." Just that one chance for a big publicity story. Like a restaurant that finally gets its publicity moment and then the restaurant is just buzzing.

From that coaching session with Marcus, we were able to deliver a ninety-day plan and execute it for one of his companies.

Also, through that experience, I found that it took me back to my Innovision company days with my old coworkers, I felt like I wasn't on the same level as the others on my team and our respective effort levels weren't matching. Between my business partner at the time and me, we had differences on views, values, respect levels, and philosophies.

Change Your Circle, Change Your Life

Ultimately, our partnership ended in December 2020.

It's like we took a giant leap forward just from that one experience with Marcus. It all comes down to mindset and going for the long haul.

Again, I don't consider myself in the championship but the next year we had the team to do it and we're going for the shiny trophy. The whole experience has expanded my mind for me to get to that next level.

As an analogy, it's like Mario from the video game, getting the mushroom. I leveled up.

Now, even without the client that Marcus gave us, we had our best month in the beginning of 2021. If you have the right mindset, you can build confidence. If you can get the confidence, you can get to the next level. Confidence builds opportunity. Opportunity leads to bigger wins, which changes your mindset.

Wins change your mindset.

And then you just continue on that circle.

Mindset → Wins ---> Opportunity → Confidence

Striving for a Championship

I used to work with one of my good friends named Jeremy McGlothlin. He coached and played college basketball for Cardinal Stretch University.

One day he told me he needed an assistant coach. I used to play back in the day and I love watching basketball. I said I could probably help so he gave me an opportunity to coach seventh and eighth graders on a summer league. What I learned from that experience was that there were kids in different places as far as basketball.

Jamar Jones

They all wanted to win but the question was, for what kind of reasons do you want to win? One kid on the team always wanted to hold the ball, drive when he wasn't supposed to, and take way too many shots. It's not that he was going for points. He just wanted to make sure he had a good game. How are you going to build up your team to win a championship if the kids aren't thinking about that? As we were going to practice and to games, I started to see the kids constantly fighting themselves with this mindset.

As soon as one kid had a good game, he would be pumped up about it even when we lost the game. Jeremy would be furious because he had that championship mindset, and it wasn't about one player's performance; it was about all of us as a collective. He would get down to the real root issue and what you need to really be thinking about.

The kid who said "I had a good game" he didn't care about. Jeremy would ask very provoking questions: Did we win? Did we run the plays like we were supposed to? You missed fifteen opportunities of wide-open players and you passed up an open teammate; why did that happen?

The kid was thinking too small. He wasn't thinking long-term success, just short-term.

We had one kid on the team who was our best shooter, but he was scared to shoot. He was the one who was thinking about others too much. Some people are afraid to take the shot and afraid for the success. You don't give yourself the opportunity to even set yourself up for long-term success. He needed to switch his fear from the negative thoughts to "I'm going to take the shot and see what happens."

Also, recognizing small wins saying "Hey, I played a great game and got the whole team involved." It's all about mindset. When you have those wins, how are you articulating them and are you on the right path?

It's all about the fundamentals that will get you to the championship.

Change Your Circle, Change Your Life

Have a process. Set up a goal. Have a plan. Run the plays. Even in the games that we lost, Jeremy congratulated all of the kids if he saw progress and effort: "Good job running the new plays! You got some good shots in! It was just an off night!" Effort on a whole team level. Examples like they did the new plays from practice. They put some good shots in but was just an off night. Effort on a whole team level.

Sometimes you may fail; however, if you follow the plan, things will fall into place.

At the end of the season, we went to a large, regional championship in Indiana. Issues they had in the middle of the season; they had perfected. Now when they had to rise to the occasion, they were ready. The kid who was overly aggressive became a team leader who brought up others. But when he needed to turn it on, he would turn it on. It was funny because at the end, he would come to us and in a way, ask permission to turn it on. He would look to us and kind of say, "Hey, can I do this?" These kids had never played to this level of basketball. We bonded together as a team and won the regional. Jeremy was a fantastic caring coach. The life lessons he is teaching these players is invaluable.

The kid who was afraid of shooting improved a little bit more but didn't break through until later on in life. I think he went on to play college ball. I think he was their #1 shooter.

Lessons/Takeaway

Don't get carried away with small-time success. Go for the championship. Go for the end goal. Go for the big win. Do you want to be the person who eats one fish a day or do you want to be the person who has a feast every day? Do you want to just feed yourself with a spear or do you want a net full for yourself and enough to feed your village? If you want to change your circle, you're going to understand that this is a long game.

If you're not practicing this continually, and going for that championship, you're not going to see the results you want to get. In your circle, right now look to see who is going for the championship and who is soaking in that one win.

Soaking in that government stimulus check. Maybe they get a good tax return. You know what I'm talking about. Look who is playing the long game in your circle as this will be a further identifier for you to evaluate. Winners roll with winners, baby. And losers roll with losers. That's just life. It all goes back to your circle.

My friend Colleen Sullivan started a new business called Sullisoaps. She started with an idea and launched within two months! She was successful in her launch for many reasons, but the main reason was her circle had a championship mindset. She launched her first day with thousands of dollars in sales Even the first month was well over three figures. She could've just taken that amazing start to her business and soaked in it. Her circle is asking her how to grow, pushing her, implementing new soaps. Her circle gave her good, quality ideas to improve on her business. She was able to do it because of the people in her circle. Not everyone can pull that off with their immediate circle right now. Could you do that with your circle?"

She built a large circle over the years and didn't know how to necessarily maximize off that network. Now she's on her way to doing better things. It's never easy, even if you have investors and a million followers. You might get a huge influx in sales but then are you able to maintain it? Can you produce it? Building a business is never easy. But it's so rewarding along the way for stories like that and when you reach your goals!

Jamar Jones

Action Items

Learn when and when not to pat yourself on the back. Keep going and keep doing it. Just because one person called you back after making twenty calls, say that's fantastic and keep going. Keep up the stamina. How much stamina do you need to overcome the challenges?

Step 1: Write down all of your life goals. As many goals as you can. Anything you want. Money, respect, influence, a big home...write it down.

Step 2: Write down why. Why do you want those things? And if your why is too bland, this is the part where you may need to dig deeper into it. Why do you want to be rich? Why do you want to be a manager? What is your "why" for keeping on going.

Step 3: Figure out how you're going to get there. Break down and write down your main goals. Then write down your goals for the next three months that add up to your overall main goal.

Step 4: Write down your first-quarter goals. What do you have to get done by halftime? Map out what you're going to do and achieve this week and then what you need to be doing on a daily basis. A weekly basis, Every three months. Annually.

(You need to repeat your three-month goals every quarter of the game)

If it's about to be halftime, you need to repeat your goals.

After you've written all your goals and planned this out to the best of your ability, you need to figure out what kind of team you need to build to meet these goals. You can't do it alone. You need an accountability partner and a structure of support.

Step 5: Get into groups and teams that will give you accountability. Make sure you track your wins and accomplishments along the way.

Change Your Circle, Change Your Life

It is hard to hold yourself accountable. Track your points because how will you know you're on the right track if you're not keeping score.

MOMENTUM

To put everything into effect, you must understand the momentum.

Let's say you start picking up a little bit of momentum. You must know how to move. It's not coasting. It's about picking up steam. Momentum is hard to start. But if you stop, it's harder to pick it up and get back in the rhythm when you resume. It's so hard to get back in the mindset.

This chapter is also about roadblocks. You're going to have things that are going to try to derail you and you must keep it going. Also, when the fire is started, how do you keep it burning? What impresses me more than someone who just starts something is someone who keeps going.

If you have been doing something for ten years, it's like, how do you continually do it? How do you keep going?

Jeff Kortes told me to always ask three questions:

• Where do you see yourself going?

• What is it going to take to get there?

• Do you want to pay the price?

I love that statement because those questions are so universal and so easy to understand.

So, for example, someone answers the first question with, "I want to be rich."

What is it going to take to get there? Do I want to pay the price?

That last question will stop most people.

131

Change Your Circle, Change Your Life

And the last question is from my good friend, Randy Wilinski: Why haven't you paid it already?

Some people do get opportunities that come up. They don't get lucky necessarily, but they get that shot and that chance. Most people don't continue the chance. They take the chance and coast. Or they take the chance and blow it. Honestly for myself, I have felt like this.

And you don't even notice it. You're not in the starting phase; you're now running. You're not walking or pacing anymore.

Foureva Media, when I was working the business, especially in year three. I still felt in the starting phase. When is it going to happen for me? I had been doing music for so many years, I built momentum, it got cut short, and I had to build the momentum up again. It's like I had to start the lawnmower in my head. I have the gas. I have everything.

What is going on? I had to figure out, is it hooked up correctly? Is it the right type of mower? What am I doing wrong? The answer was, just keep going.

You keep doing what you need to do until it is your time. Until it is your time for your lawnmower to start, for your car to go. So, I did a few more years of trying but not feeling off the ground. Then in year five, that is when I realized that the engines were going, I was already driving. I had been trying to start the car for so long and I realized I was already going. It's always something you don't initially feel but you must keep going.

How do you keep it going? You get knocked down; you encounter roadblocks. Organization, goal setting and surrounding yourself with the right circle will keep the fire going. If you don't have those three things, you'll get derailed, and it'll be hard to start again. If you're in the beginning phase, think about how hard it was for you to actually start.

Jamar Jones

Once you develop momentum, you don't want to lose it. Something pops up unplanned; you have to ask yourself; do you want to go back to the start? There is no way. Once you pick up steam, that is when it says, "Oh, you really want this? All right. Let's line it up." And you have to trust in yourself, trust the process.

You said you wanted to pay the price. It's time to pay up.

The goal is to get where someone else is driving you and someone else is operating and driving it for you and you're getting chauffeured. Momentum will take old problems that used to be tough for you. The key is to pick up enough speed to be plowing through. You'll start to blow past the smaller challenges. There will be larger challenges down the road, but you're starting to see results and now you're seeing them on a regular basis.

Momentum will carry itself depending on how fast you're going. And that is one benefit. Anything you're doing will keep moving forward. But you eventually have to give it more gas. Unless you're going downhill.

Even in music, when I slowed down with it, I still had a few gigs just because people still knew of me. This DJ I knew called me up and said come do some songs. If you want to get where you want to go, you have to start doing it, so you get known for it. You have to be the person who delivers and has a portfolio of your work. The more people see you doing it, the more people will recommend you and it will build the momentum for you. I did shows. Then opportunities started to appear. And that is why my album was called *Momentum*. I would open for major artists. I didn't have to pay. I opened for Yellow Wolf, a couple people at the Rave. It was all because I picked up momentum. And then it was easier to keep going and it wasn't having to reinvent the wheel.

The hardest part is when it goes from an idea to a couple of concepts. But that growing pain needs to happen. You can't just be a talker and have an idea. If you're just out there talking about it, how can people know that you're the one for the job?

Momentum is a great feeling when you're in it, but it is a test of, "Do you really want this?" You could just stop but it's almost harder to stop. You have responsibility and accountability. Then it boils down to how bad do you want it.

How bad do you want to reach your goals? Reaching them always sounds amazing and like pure bliss. But the reality hits you quickly and you really have to say, how bad do I want this to happen?

Do you really want it or do you just kind of want it? A lot of people have dreams of being top of the top. They want millions. They want rich people problems.

They may even say, "Oh, I would kill for that," Would you? What would you do to get there?

For a lot of those people, it took a lot to get there.

But are they really willing to pay whatever price it takes to get there? A lot of people are not. Now that you've committed, you have to continue. It's hard enough to start; it's really tough to continue. Yes, you don't have to start the car over and over, but you have to keep it running. And even when you reach your goal, nine times out of ten, it's not going to be this blissful achievement.

Grass isn't always greener on the other side. You'll have different problems to worry about. More pressure.

When you start something, the pressure is sometimes lighter. Yes, you might need it to be successful as you have no other option. The pressure gets more intense the more you get into momentum. You can't back out now; you're in it.

You have people relying on you; the stakes are higher. If you're just starting something and you fail, "Okay, I can just go back and get a job again." But the higher the stakes, the more the pressure intensifies.

Your goal has to be something that is somewhat of a concern. Ask yourself how bad you really want to achieve what you're trying to achieve.

The only person you can blame is yourself. Because if you're not in the spot where you want to be at, you didn't want it bad enough. You found excuses, cop-outs. This is on you. You can't blame and complain about every single thing that is out of your hands.

It's about the journey of pursuit and your endurance. Do you have the stamina to keep going? Most people don't. They value other things more than their dreams.

And they're not willing to pay the price. It's sad but it's true. Most people will make excuses. Why not me?

You have to pay the toll. You better find a way. Your circle can be rocket fuel for your dreams. To get you that momentum and pick-up speed faster. Or it can be rocks and anchors dragging you down to the bottom of the sea. It doesn't matter what you do/ Until you change that circle, you don't have a chance. The circle will help hold you accountable to reach your goals. It's like a push notification on your phone.

That is your accountability group. That's your circle. "Hey, you said you were doing this. How did it go? What happened with that?" They check up, ask questions. The other side of that is having a circle of people undermining what you're doing, saying it is a waste of time. They pull you back from where you're trying to go.

Here is a secret: If you have the right circles in place to propel you to your goals and dreams, you can pick up speed quickly. Get a team to build momentum. Get a team because you can't do it yourself. You need the accountability and the fire power around you. You can start but to really get where you're trying to go, you need the squad.

Action Items

When you have momentum, you've got to iron out the creases. Now that you've got momentum, you need to sustain it. The only way to sustain it is to keep remembering the bottom line. Like in basketball, you've got momentum and you're winning games. How do you keep it going? By practicing shots, strengthening the defense. It's not about the fancy layups, not about scoring the most points, learning something new. It's about going back to your roots and sharpening your existing skills that created your momentum in the first place.

With my company, I feel as if our momentum is going but as we grow, we need to make sure that we're not just focusing on innovation. Some companies find initial success (maybe some press) and they go downhill after their original boom because their customer service was garbage. So now they have a bunch of negative reviews. They have to start over. Stick to what is working and double down on it. Get back to the fundamentals. Make note of processes, procedures, how to make it scalable.

Step 1: Identify (when you're picking up momentum in whatever you're doing) the top three things that led you to this point: We finally got the right team. Someone promoted my business. I got help from someone.

Step 2: Write down ways that you can sustain or duplicate that success. What are you going to do to maintain that?

Say one product is a crowd favorite with your customers. If the team got you there, how are you going to keep the team? If an investor got you there, how are you going to keep the investor? Reinvest in the success. Identify the things you're doing well that are "winning" that you're going to sustain.

Step 3: Identify three things that you can innovate. Identify your weaknesses or areas where you're not "winning." Innovate on your weaknesses. Figure out smart solutions to them. Maybe you need to find a new manufacturer. We're growing and the lead time is not matching up with demand. You need to work on identifying a new partnership with a new manufacturer. The key is to identify your weaknesses and, as you gain momentum, don't get lazy, or complacent, or cocky.

Look at the fundamentals and see what it is going to take to keep the momentum going. These tools and questions will help you to address the roadblocks that will kill your momentum.

When I look at how I got here, the common theme was that I changed my circle, which changed my situation, which changed my outcome. I realized I needed to change my circle probably when I was about twenty-one or twenty-two. I realized I needed to change how I went about things. Back when I was fifteen- to twenty-years old, I was an angry person. I didn't see any good in the world. I was skeptical. I acted first, asked questions later. I was judgmental and reactionary. I hung out with the wrong people.

I was running in the wrong circles. My focus was deterred by things that truly didn't matter. I didn't see a way out except through music. I had pushed away certain friends and family who were only trying to see the best in me. I wasn't in any mentally stable place to accept who I was or to have self-awareness. Dealing with a lot of racial issues and intentions, different groups of kids who were challenging me every day. My anger was so bad, I had visited different pastors, therapists, and school counselors to find the help.

My parents were giving me outlets to discuss next steps. How do I get out of this? What's the path? When you talk about someone who was "broken," I resonate and feel for the people who were or are in my previous situation. That's how I know that, coming from that mindset, I was able to change my life from that standpoint by changing my circle.

I know this works if you apply all of the principles. Forcibly changing my circle (moving high school to high school) made me restart which path I was on. I was ripped out of the environment so I couldn't continue down that same road.

If you look at this book and think "This is a lot to do," then refuse to do these things, well, I have a message for you. If you want to be a rock and stuck and do the same things, then stay there. This book isn't for you. This book isn't for someone who wants to stay stagnant.

This book is for someone who wants to do something about their life. It is for people who want to get ahead, who are unhappy with their current situation. This book is to empower you to take action and to grow your mindset to achieve anything possible. There is no limit to this book. It's a cliché to say but this book shows you how to do it. It is the key to opening any door and walking through it.

Apply the lessons from this book repeatedly to your life, over and over again. Revisit each chapter. Figure out the key principles and methods you need to work on and apply them. Then go back and use them as a roadmap over and over again. Just by reading this book and applying all of the actionable methods and how-to's, you've already changed your life. You need to keep evaluating and changing because you need to keep the momentum going.

Now go and Change your Circle; Change your Life.

☼ ABOUT THE AUTHOR: ☼

I'm a visionary that believes in Leadership and that we can connect with one another in a relatable way.

My path has been nothing but easy. From my decision making and the search of finding myself, I've had many hardships in my life that I've overcome. I've created many things from just a thought and once I put my mind to something there's nothing that can stop me.

Going from a very angry individual, experienced racism as a teenager, went to four different high schools in three different states, feeling lost and not knowing exactly where I wanted to go. Having a thriving music career for over a decade and then losing my voice. Went through a heartbreaking divorce, to building my own business from the ground up now having a team of people working for my communications and marketing agency, Foureva Media.

Anything's possible. Looking back, I've learned that there were elements to my success, one of the main ones was the circle I was in and how to get into other circles. I've applied this methodology in my personal life and in business.

My change started with me and the people that I was around.

The question is are you ready?

Are you ready to change your perspective and unlock your greatness?